# The Self-love Mindset

# The Self-love Mindset

## Why Personal Well-being Is the Ultimate Business Strategy

# Lauri-Ann Ainsworth

CAPSTONE
A Wiley Brand

*Registered Office(s)*
John Wiley & Sons, Inc., 111 River Street, Hoboken, NJ 07030, USA
John Wiley & Sons Ltd, The Atrium, Southern Gate, Chichester, West Sussex, PO19 8SQ, UK

*Editorial Office*
The Atrium, Southern Gate, Chichester, West Sussex, PO19 8SQ, UK

For details of our global editorial offices, customer services, and more information about Wiley products visit us at www.wiley.com.

Wiley also publishes its books in a variety of electronic formats and by print-on-demand. Some content that appears in standard print versions of this book may not be available in other formats. Designations used by companies to distinguish their products are often claimed as trademarks. All brand names and product names used in this book are trade names, service marks, trademarks or registered trademarks of their respective owners. The publisher is not associated with any product or vendor mentioned in this book.

*Limit of Liability/Disclaimer of Warranty*
While the publisher and authors have used their best efforts in preparing this work, they make no representations or warranties with respect to the accuracy or completeness of the contents of this work and specifically disclaim all warranties, including without limitation any implied warranties of merchantability or fitness for a particular purpose. No warranty may be created or extended by sales representatives, written sales materials or promotional statements for this work. The fact that an organization, website, or product is referred to in this work as a citation and/or potential source of further information does not mean that the publisher and authors endorse the information or services the organization, website, or product may provide or recommendations it may make. This work is sold with the understanding that the publisher is not engaged in rendering professional services. The advice and strategies contained herein may not be suitable for your situation. You should consult with a specialist where appropriate. Further, readers should be aware that websites listed in this work may have changed or disappeared between when this work was written and when it is read. Neither the publisher nor authors shall be liable for any loss of profit or any other commercial damages, including but not limited to special, incidental, consequential, or other damages.

*Library of Congress Cataloging-in-Publication Data is Available:*

ISBN 9781907312779 (Paperback)
ISBN 9781907312793 (ePDF)
ISBN 9781907312786 (ePub)

Cover Design: Wiley
Cover Image: © pixelrobot/Adobe Stock
Author Photo: Courtesy of the Author

SKY10097970_020625

*To my dearest Savannah and Sebastian,*

*You are my greatest teachers and my biggest inspiration. Savannah, with your songs and stories that bring life to every moment, and Sebastian, with your endless curiosity and love for numbers, you both remind me every day what it means to truly know and love yourself.*

*This book is not only for the world, but for you. It carries the lessons I hope you live by: to love yourselves first, to know yourself deeply, and to create value that extends far beyond your presence. Remember that self-love is the foundation upon which you can build a life of purpose, joy, and impact.*

*With all my love,*

*Mom*

# Contents

# Acknowledgements

This book is the culmination of a deeply personal journey, and it wouldn't have been possible without the love, support, and encouragement of so many incredible people in my life.

First and foremost, to my children, Savannah and Sebastian – you are my heart and soul. Watching you grow has been one of my greatest joys, and it is for you that I strive to embody the principles of self-love and self-awareness every day. Thank you for being my inspiration, my motivation, and my reason for continuing this journey.

To my family, who has always stood by me, especially during the times when I struggled to find my way – you have been my anchors. Thank you for your unwavering belief in me, even when I doubted myself.

To my friends and colleagues at the Branson Centre of Entrepreneurship, thank you for your constant support and for believing in my vision. Your encouragement, collaboration, and dedication to the work we do have been invaluable. This book reflects the passion and purpose we bring to our mission every day.

To my mentors, who have guided me with wisdom and grace – your insights have been instrumental in shaping the person I am today. You've taught me the importance of showing up as my true self and leading from a place of authenticity.

Finally, to my readers, thank you for embarking on this journey with me. It is my hope that the lessons in these pages inspire you to love yourself, know yourself, and create value that extends far beyond your own life.

With gratitude,
Lauri-Ann

# About the Author

**Lauri-Ann Ainsworth** is the CEO of the Richard Branson Centre of Entrepreneurship Caribbean, a business leader, coach, and speaker with a passion for empowering individuals to unlock their true potential. With over a decade of experience in entrepreneurship and leadership, Lauri-Ann has dedicated her career to fostering innovation and building ecosystems that support entrepreneurs across the Caribbean.

Her personal journey of overcoming self-doubt, burnout, and limiting beliefs led her to develop *The Self-love Mindset* – a transformative philosophy that teaches individuals to love themselves through self-care, know themselves through self-awareness, and create lasting value through service. Lauri-Ann's work blends her experience as a leader with her personal commitment to well-being, offering practical strategies for personal and professional success.

A mother of two, Lauri-Ann believes in leading by example, showing her children and those around her the importance of self-love, authenticity, and resilience. Through her writing, coaching, and public speaking, she is on a mission to inspire others to live a life of purpose, fulfilment, and true self-awareness.

# **Introduction**

I believe we all want the same thing in life: happiness and fulfilment. We want to thrive – in life and in business – and to know that our lives matter. We want to wake up every day with a reason to take on the day. But why is it that most people don't attain it? Most people stay stuck in survival mode, just getting by. Whether it's being stuck in a job that doesn't inspire them, a relationship that no longer feels right, or simply living in a way that doesn't align with who they are, many people end up chasing what they perceive to be fulfilment – accomplishments, credentials, titles – but at the end of the day, they still feel unfulfilled. I believe that fulfilment is achieved by using our strengths to solve a problem that matters to us in service to others.

So, what keeps people in this cycle of just existing? It's chaos and confusion. These forces keep us disconnected from the life we truly want, from doing work or living in ways that bring us joy. They keep us from finding the fulfilment and happiness we crave.

When chaos and confusion take over, you feel stuck. There's no direction. Procrastination sets in. You chase shiny objects, feel like an imposter, and your to-do list never seems to shrink. Days pass, and it feels like you've accomplished nothing. Life feels reactive, like you're just responding to whatever comes your way instead of living with intention. Relationships start to suffer, and the constant stress, exhaustion, and anxiety become your norm.

Have you ever thought about reinventing yourself because, deep down, you know something has to change? Most of us reach that point eventually – when we're just over it. Over the job that drains us, the relationship that's no longer working, or the routine that numbs us. It's that moment when the nagging feeling that there's more for you becomes too loud to ignore, but you can't quite figure out how to get there. It's when you're ready to stop blaming others, your circumstances, or even yourself for the life you don't want. It's when you decide to stop being a passenger and take control of your own story.

This is where the shift begins – moving from merely surviving to truly thriving. Chaos and confusion are often what keep us stuck, trapped in cycles of stress and dissatisfaction. They prevent us from seeing clearly and from making decisions that truly align with who we are and what we want. But when we take 100% responsibility for our happiness, fulfilment, and well-being, that's when the fog starts to lift. Personal well-being isn't a luxury or something to prioritize only when life slows down – it's the foundation for everything. When we cultivate balance, self-care, and self-awareness, we begin to see through the chaos and confusion, allowing us to show up differently in both life and business. This is why personal well-being is the ultimate business strategy – it clears the path for real, sustainable success.

# Why Is Personal Well-being the Ultimate Business Strategy?

In a world where the demands of business are relentless, the idea that personal well-being is the ultimate business strategy might seem counter-intuitive. Yet, it is becoming increasingly clear that the foundation of sustainable success lies not in the endless pursuit of external goals but in the cultivation of inner balance and self-love. At the heart of this concept is the self-love mindset – a philosophy that embraces self-care, self-awareness, and service as the pillars of personal and professional well-being. At the core of this philosophy is the belief that true success begins with taking 100% responsibility for our own happiness, fulfilment, and well-being. I believe that this responsibility goes far beyond individual benefits as it impacts the collective success of organizations and communities.

From the individual perspective, prioritizing personal well-being is not merely an act of self-indulgence; it's a strategic choice that fuels productivity, creativity, and resilience. When we care for our bodies through proper nutrition, exercise, and rest, we equip ourselves with the energy needed to tackle the challenges of the day. Self-awareness allows us to navigate our emotions, align our actions with our core values, and maintain a sense of purpose, even in the face of adversity. By being in tune with our needs and boundaries, we can prevent burnout, make better decisions, and bring our best selves to our work.

For organizations, the benefits of fostering personal well-being among employees are equally important. Companies that encourage a culture of self-care and self-awareness not only see reduced absenteeism and healthcare costs but also benefit from a more engaged and motivated workforce. When employees feel valued and supported in their personal growth, they are more likely to be innovative, collaborative, and committed to the company's mission. The pillar of service within the self-love mindset emphasizes that the greatest value we can offer to others stems from our own well-cared-for selves. This creates a positive cyclical effect where personal and organizational success are deeply intertwined.

Ultimately, the self-love mindset challenges the traditional, often toxic, notions of success that prioritize external achievements over internal fulfilment. It invites both individuals and organizations to redefine success as a state of holistic well-being, where self-care, self-awareness, and service to others are not just personal virtues but strategic imperatives. By embracing this mindset, we recognize that the first step in creating value in the world and in the workplace is to create value within ourselves. Only when we take full responsibility for our own well-being can we truly be of service to others and drive meaningful, sustainable success in our professional lives.

Many of us, whether we're leaders in an organization, employees, or entrepreneurs, know what it feels like to be trapped in our own lives, endlessly spinning on a hamster wheel without ever really getting anywhere.

Work, which takes up the majority of our waking hours, plays a massive role in this feeling of disconnection. For many employees, workplaces demand speed and constant achievement, often at the expense of meaningful engagement and personal growth. It's no wonder that so many people feel like they're just cogs in a machine, mechanically going through the motions without a true connection to their work.

This sense of disengagement is widespread. Many employees are showing up physically, but mentally, they've already checked out. They're at their desks, but their minds are elsewhere. It's a phenomenon often referred to as 'quiet quitting', where people do the bare minimum just to get by. I can remember being in this zone myself, and the feeling of living on autopilot without being at the wheel was my reality for many years.

Stress levels tell a similar story. Employees around the world continue to report record levels of stress, with many feeling overwhelmed by the relentless pace of modern work. It's a problem that's been building for years and affects not just employees, but entrepreneurs too.

For entrepreneurs, the pressure can be just as intense. The constant need to innovate, meet market demands, and stay ahead of the competition is often overwhelming. While entrepreneurship promises freedom, it can feel like a double-edged sword, with every decision resting on your shoulders. In the pursuit of success, many entrepreneurs find themselves sacrificing their well-being and losing sight of why they started in the first place.

Whether you're working for a company or paving your own way as an entrepreneur, when most of your time feels empty of purpose or satisfaction, it's easy to feel stuck. When that stuck feeling settles in, it doesn't just stay at work – it seeps into every other area of life, reinforcing the sensation that you're caught in an endless, aimless loop.

While more organizations are beginning to recognize the importance of workplace well-being, there's one crucial piece that often gets missed: **it all starts with the individual.**

How do I know all of this?

Well, I'm not a psychologist, and I'm certainly not an expert in organizational behaviour. The truth is, I learned it the hard way – by going through my own journey of burnout and finding my way back. I've always believed that the most valuable advice comes from those who have actually walked the path you're on. I went through a transformational chapter in my life, and honestly, I'm still on that journey because I believe we're all constantly evolving and growing.

During that transformation, I found myself where most transformational stories begin – at rock bottom. What I'm sharing in this book is everything I learned on my climb back up. My hope is that by sharing my message, it will reach the people who need to hear it, in the way they need to hear it. Now, let me be clear – there's nothing groundbreaking or brand new in this book. If you're looking for some revolutionary technique, I won't pretend I've discovered one. What I have done is taken all the lessons, tools, and insights I've gathered and distilled them into something that may be easier to understand and put into action. It certainly was for me.

This is my way of giving back – by sharing what worked for me and has helped others too. The methods, information, and techniques I talk about are all backed by solid scientific research, but what sets this apart is how I approach putting all that knowledge into practice.

## Burnout and Back

When I found myself burnt out and depleted, I was completely confused about what to do next, and I wanted to make sense of what I was going through.

I was always a motivated and inspired person, so when I found myself living on autopilot and feeling completely dejected about my life, I couldn't process any complicated information.

I was looking for simple steps – something that would help me start that climb up from rock bottom. That's what *The Self-love Mindset* is all about. It's part memoir, part collection of everything I've researched and put into practice for myself.

This book dives deep into the steps I took and how. Sure, being overworked is one thing, but it's how we tend to our inner flame that really determines whether it flickers out or keeps burning strong. I hope you'll stick with me throughout this journey we are about to embark on as I'm sure there may be a nugget of wisdom or a new way of thinking that can support you as you navigate your life – both personally and professionally.

# 1

# The Self-love Journey: A Framework for Personal Transformation

*To love oneself is the beginning of a lifelong romance.*
– Oscar Wilde

As I moved through my healing journey, I realized that true change doesn't come from constantly striving or pushing through burnout. It comes from understanding that the most important relationship you have is the one with yourself. This became the foundation of my transformation – a new approach to life centred around self-love. The more I prioritized my own well-being, the more clarity, energy, and peace I gained. That's when I understood that loving yourself isn't a luxury – it's essential if you want to thrive, not just survive.

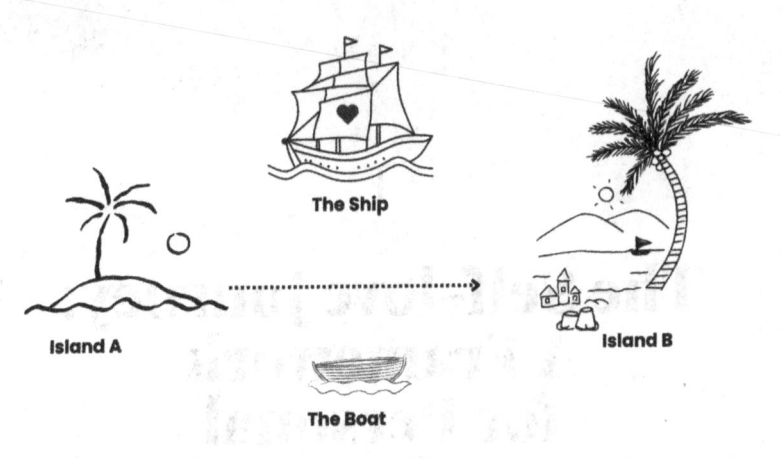

**Figure 1: The Self-Love Mindset Journey** – A visual representation of the transformative path from Island A, symbolizing our current life mode, to Island B, a space of growth and fulfillment. The boat and ship illustrate the different stages and tools we use along the way.

This led me to the Self-love Mindset, a way of thinking and living that helps us navigate life with intention, less stress, and a deeper sense of fulfilment. This framework is built on three pillars.

# Self-care | Self-awareness | Service

So, let's talk about two islands, a boat, and a ship!

What does that have to do with anything? Stick with me as I explain. Since we're all on a journey, it makes sense that we have a starting point, a destination, and different ways to get there. We're always looking to move from where we are now to somewhere else – whether that's a better version of ourselves, a new goal, or a different life circumstance. Picture yourself on Island A – this represents your current life, where you are right now. But, you want to get to Island B – your desired future, your goals, dreams, or the vision you have for yourself.

Now, you have two ways to make that journey. You could take a small boat. But this boat is unstable, and the waters are rough, making the journey turbulent and exhausting. The boat represents the habits, thoughts, and patterns that keep you stuck – constantly paddling but never making real progress. It's draining and leaves you stressed about whether you'll even reach your destination.

Or, you could board the ship. This ship is bigger, steady, and equipped with everything that makes the journey enjoyable – comfort, relaxation, and even some fun. The ship represents the Self-love Mindset. It's about how you choose to navigate your life's journey. Instead of stressing about getting to Island B as quickly as possible, the ship allows you to enjoy the journey itself. Growth and change are inevitable, but what matters most isn't just reaching your destination; it's how you travel, how you care for yourself along the way, and how much joy, peace, and fulfilment you allow yourself to experience.

This mindset helps you stop obsessing over the outcome and start appreciating the steps you're taking to get there. It's about embracing the ups and downs because that's where real transformation happens.

This journey is one we all take, but it's important to remember that no one can walk it for you. It's as unique as you are. Too often, we go through life as passengers, simply observing instead of steering the ship and being intentional about the direction we want to head in.

You might be living as if you have no control over your circumstances, feeling like life is just happening to you. I've been there – thinking I had to accept whatever was handed to me, falling into the mindset of being a victim of my circumstances. But eventually, I couldn't stay in that space any longer. That's when I realized I didn't just need to reinvent myself – I needed to rediscover who I truly was.

# 2
# Understanding Your Life Modes

*Your life does not get better by chance, it gets better by change.*

– Jim Rohn

I began to realize that true transformation doesn't happen by accident – it requires understanding where we are in our journey. Before I could figure out where I wanted to go, I needed to know what my starting point was. Understanding where you are in your journey is crucial for growth. Often, we feel stuck or overwhelmed with no clear path. When I discovered John Maxwell's *The Power of Significance*, it introduced me to the concept of life modes. Life modes are the different stages or states we move through as we navigate our personal and professional journeys. They represent how we engage with the world at any given time – whether we're simply surviving, seeking stability, building security, or striving for significance. Each mode reflects a different level of awareness and action, and understanding which one you're in currently is key to knowing how to move forward.

For example, in **Survival Mode**, life feels reactive. You're in crisis-management mode, doing whatever it takes to make it through the day. There's little room for reflection or growth because you're so focused on meeting your basic needs. It's exhausting, and it often feels like you're treading water with no end in sight.

When you shift into **Stability Mode**, things start to feel more manageable. You've found a rhythm that allows you to meet your needs consistently, but there's still a sense that something's missing. You might feel comfortable, but you're not yet thriving. It's a period of consolidation – where you focus on routines and creating a sense of balance, but you may not yet be chasing your larger dreams.

In **Security Mode**, you've built a solid foundation. You're no longer just surviving or getting by; you feel confident and in control. There's an emerging desire for more meaning and fulfilment, and you start seeking alignment between your daily actions and your deeper values. You begin asking, 'What's next? What's truly important to me?'

Finally, **Significance Mode** is where transformation really takes hold. In this mode, you've discovered a sense of purpose and are contributing to something greater than yourself. You're making an impact in your work, relationships, or community, and this brings a deep sense of fulfilment. You're no longer just focused on personal success – you're creating value that extends beyond your own life.

Each of these life modes represents a step in your journey, and they help you understand where you are and what you need to do next. There's no judgment in which mode you're in – it's about awareness. Once you know where you are, you can begin taking intentional steps to move towards the life you truly want to live. Understanding your current life mode is like looking at a map: you can't reach your destination until you know your starting point.

In my own journey, I realized that these life modes are fluid and cyclical, like a spiral. Often I thought I had reached stability or security, only to be thrown back into survival mode by an unexpected event – a financial setback, a personal crisis, or a health issue. At first, this felt frustrating, as if I was failing at making progress. But over time, I began to understand that these setbacks are part of the process. Life modes aren't linear, and they're not a reflection of failure. Instead, they're opportunities for growth and a reminder that progress is about learning to navigate life with resilience, not perfection.

This isn't just about moving towards our destinations, it's about how we evolve. Each mode presents its own set of challenges and lessons, and moving from one to another is about developing the right tools – self-care and self-awareness – to help you along the way.

# Self-care and Self-awareness as Tools for Growth

I believe these four stages of life can be mapped in a matrix that reflects how much we love and know ourselves. Figure 2 illustrates the relationship between high and low self-love and self-awareness, showing how these elements intersect to influence your life mode. Life modes are not fixed destinations – they ebb and flow depending on where you are in your journey. The

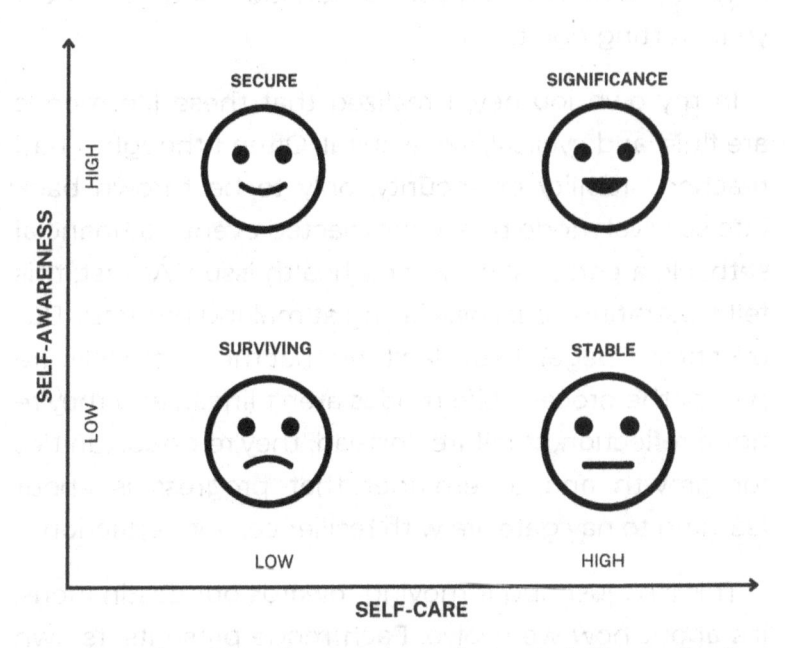

**Figure 2: The Life Modes Matrix** – A framework illustrating how we move from survival to significance where we are thriving. The X-axis represents self-care, while the Y-axis represents self-awareness. Together, they form four distinct life modes, guiding us toward a balanced and fulfilling state of being.

balance between self-care and self-awareness is key to understanding which mode you are currently in and how to progress forward.

Self-care allows us to meet our basic needs, while self-awareness leads to intentional growth and clarity. By improving both, we can navigate the complexities of life with greater ease. In the upcoming chapters, we'll explore these concepts further, revealing how nurturing yourself through self-care and expanding your self-awareness can shift you into higher life modes. This work enables you to rise above the chaos and confusion that may be holding you back and move towards a more purposeful and fulfilling life.

# Life Modes Assessment: Where Are You on Your Journey?

Now that you've explored the concept of life modes, it's time to reflect on where you currently are on your journey. This assessment is designed to help you understand which life mode you are in based on how you are currently experiencing life. Take a few moments to read each statement and consider how much it resonates with your current situation.

For each statement, rate yourself from 1 to 5: 1 = This rarely applies to me to 5 = This applies to me often. For each life mode, tally your score based on your responses (from 1 to 5 for each statement). Your total score for each mode should fall within a range that helps you determine where you are.

Add up your total score for each life mode.

- 5–10 points: You're likely not in this life mode.

- 11–15 points: You might be in the early stages of this life mode.

- 16–25 points: You're strongly in this life mode.

## Survival Mode

- I feel overwhelmed by my daily tasks and often struggle to meet my basic needs (like sleep, nutrition, or stress management).

- I often feel like I'm putting out fires and reacting to emergencies rather than planning ahead.

- My energy is low, and I'm frequently exhausted, mentally or physically.

- I don't feel like I have time for self-care, and when I do, it feels like a luxury I can't afford.

- I have a hard time reflecting on what I need or what I want out of life.

## Stability Mode

- I have a routine in place that makes life more predictable and manageable.

- I can meet my basic needs without feeling as overwhelmed as I used to.

- I'm able to dedicate some time to self-care, though it's not always consistent.

- Life feels stable, but I sometimes feel like something is missing or that I'm stuck in a routine.

- I've started to think more about what I want next in life but haven't taken concrete steps yet.

**Security Mode**

- I feel confident and in control of most areas of my life, but I'm starting to seek more meaning and fulfilment.

- I've identified some of my core strengths, values, and passions, and I want to align my life with them.

- I'm able to take better care of myself physically and emotionally, and I'm more aware of what I need to feel balanced.

- I'm starting to ask deeper questions about who I am and what I'm capable of.

- I feel ready for growth and change, but I'm unsure what my next step should be.

**Significance Mode**

- I feel deeply aligned with my values and purpose, and I'm contributing to something bigger than myself.

- I'm making a meaningful impact in my work, relationships, or personal life, and it feels fulfilling.

- I'm able to balance self-care with serving others, without feeling burnt out.

- I feel a sense of peace and purpose in my daily life, knowing that I'm living authentically.

- I'm constantly growing and evolving, and I feel excited about my future.

# Interpreting Your Results

Remember that this is just a litmus test but ultimately you must discern where you believe you are. A simple assessment like this can't determine the nuances of your life. But this can give you some insights into where you may be. If you find that you have similar scores across all the life modes, it may indicate that you're transitioning between different stages. For example, if your scores for both survival and stability modes are high, you may still be working your way out of survival mode and into stability. Similarly, high scores for stability and security could suggest that you've built a stable foundation but are beginning to seek more meaning and security in your life.

Wherever you find yourself, know that this is just one stage in your ongoing journey. Life is fluid, and moving from one phase to the next requires intention, self-care, and self-awareness.

# 3

# Vision for Your Future: Moving from Island A to Island B

*Go confidently in the direction of your dreams! Live the life you've imagined.*

— Henry David Thoreau

Now that you have a better understanding of where you are – on Island A, it's time to dream about Island B. Island B represents your future desires, the evolving vision you have for your life. But here's the thing: we often think of Island B as a list of goals, achievements, or things we need to accomplish. While setting goals can be helpful, the challenge is that once we reach them, Island B becomes our new Island A. We find ourselves constantly shifting gears, setting new desires, and chasing new goals.

Island B isn't just about ticking off goals, accomplishments, or reaching a certain status – it's about something deeper. It's about how you want to feel when you get there. The real purpose of moving towards Island B isn't simply achieving a specific goal, but experiencing feelings of fulfilment, alignment, joy, and purpose along the way. This shift in focus, from external achievements to internal emotional states, is a game changer.

We often get caught up in chasing material goals, thinking they will bring us happiness. We tell ourselves, 'When I get that promotion, I'll feel secure', or, 'When I finally buy that house, I'll be happy.' But what we're really after isn't the job title or the house – it's the feeling we think those things will bring. We're not chasing things; we're chasing the emotions behind them.

The trouble is, when we put all our energy into achieving something external, we rarely stop to consider whether that thing will actually bring the feelings we desire. Often, we reach a milestone and, instead of feeling fulfilled, we feel … underwhelmed. The joy is fleeting. We celebrate for a moment and then immediately start looking for the next thing. Why? Because we haven't truly connected to the feelings we were seeking in the first place.

For me, this realization hit hard after I spent years chasing external milestones in every area of my life. When I first entered the corporate world, I believed that climbing the ladder would bring me the validation and sense of accomplishment I craved. I worked late nights, missed important moments with friends and family, and constantly pushed myself to say yes to every opportunity. When I finally got the promotion and the salary increase I had worked so hard for, I expected to feel secure and fulfilled – but that feeling never came.

The same pattern repeated itself when I transitioned into entrepreneurship. I thought that being my own boss, working on my terms, and building something from scratch would give me the freedom and satisfaction I had been missing in the corporate world. But instead of feeling liberated, I found myself caught in a whirlwind of deadlines, constantly putting out fires, and feeling more overwhelmed than ever.

It didn't stop there. I thought if I kept learning, kept gaining credentials, I would finally feel accomplished. I chased after every certification and course, believing that the next one would be the key to feeling qualified and worthy. But each time I finished a programme, I immediately found myself signing up for another one, hoping that the next credential would bring the sense of validation I was desperately seeking. It became a never-ending cycle – more courses, more certifications, more achievements – yet the feeling I was chasing remained just out of reach.

That's when I realized the issue wasn't the job, the business, or even the credentials. The truth was, I wasn't chasing the things themselves – I was chasing the feelings I thought they would bring. I was seeking validation, and a sense of worth, but I was looking for them in external achievements. No matter how much I accomplished, it was never enough because I hadn't truly connected with what I was really seeking inside.

But here's the big question: why do we treat our future selves like a checklist of goals, thinking that ticking them off will bring us happiness and fulfilment? I used to live my life exactly like that for as long as I can remember. Every year, I'd carefully curate a list of things I wanted to achieve – bucket-list style. Don't get me wrong, I still love planning and goal-setting. I see the value in setting goals, especially in business, where strategy and targets help keep us focused and guide our actions.

That approach works well for a company that measures success by hitting key performance indicators, but as individuals, we're so much more complex. Our sense of satisfaction and fulfilment doesn't usually come from simply completing a project or reaching a goal. Sure, accomplishment feels good. Real fulfilment runs deeper, and it's rarely tied to just checking off boxes.

# The Power of Focusing on Feelings

On my journey to understand myself better and the feelings driving my actions, I came across Danielle LaPorte's book *The Desire Map*. It completely shifted my perspective on goal setting. Instead of focusing on traditional goals, LaPorte introduced the idea of 'core desired feelings' – a concept that resonated deeply with me.

What if, instead of chasing arbitrary goals, we focused on how we want to feel in our lives every day? This thought was intriguing. Through a series of exercises,

I identified my core desired feelings: ease, creativity, simplicity, and nourishment. These weren't just abstract ideas – they became the blueprint for how I wanted to live my life.

That's when I realized something crucial: the goal itself wasn't going to give me the feeling I was after. What I really wanted wasn't more achievements or projects – it was the emotional states I hadn't been paying attention to. I wanted ease, creativity, simplicity, and peace. But the work I was doing? It didn't provide any of that. The process of achieving those external markers of success was actually draining me, not fulfilling me.

That realization completely shifted my approach. I stopped focusing on what I thought I should be doing and started asking myself: How do I want to feel? I started to reconnect with my core desired feelings. Rather than chasing accomplishments, I began to shape my days around those feelings of ease and creativity. It wasn't about getting to Island B as quickly as possible anymore; it was about feeling good throughout the journey.

When we focus on feelings rather than just accomplishments, the entire journey changes. It becomes less about the end result and more about how we live our lives every day. The pursuit of Island B is no longer about hitting a milestone but about cultivating the emotional states we want to experience daily – whether that's joy, peace, balance, or contribution. When we centre our actions around how we want to feel, we give ourselves permission to live in the present moment with intention, rather than postponing happiness until we 'get there'.

Your vision for the next stage of your life is deeply influenced by your current life mode. In survival, your focus may simply be on finding stability and peace, while in other stages, you might dream of personal growth or making an impact. It's important to acknowledge that your vision evolves as your circumstances change.

While dreaming big has value, it can also feel overwhelming and lead to paralysis. That's what I experienced. The idea of my grandest vision was something I needed to have as an aspiration, but I also needed some baby steps to get me there. Instead of focusing on the biggest outcome, I started to take manageable steps forward. Each small step built momentum, allowing my vision to evolve and grow naturally as I progressed. This approach gave me the balance between dreaming big and staying grounded in what I could achieve next.

Now that you've reflected on the importance of how you want to feel in your life, it's time to dive into practical activities that will help you identify your vision for the future. These exercises are designed to guide you in discovering what you truly want, not just in terms of goals, but in terms of the emotions and feelings you want to experience daily. Let's take a moment to explore these methods and shape your journey ahead.

# Creating a Feel-Good Plan

A powerful exercise that transformed how I approached my days was checking in with myself every morning – not by diving headfirst into my to-do list or worrying about the endless tasks ahead, but by asking a much more intentional question: How do I want to feel today?

Instead of starting with a long list of goals or obligations that often lead to stress and overwhelm, I began shifting the focus inward. I realized that while we often think about what we want to accomplish, we rarely take the time to consider how we want to feel while doing it. And the truth is, the way we feel directly impacts how we move through our day, the quality of our work, and our sense of fulfilment.

By asking myself this simple question each morning – 'How do I want to feel today?' – I was no longer chasing arbitrary goals for the sake of productivity. Instead, I was aligning my actions with my emotional well-being. I began to consciously think about the feelings I wanted to cultivate: Was it a sense of peace? Creativity? Confidence? Joy?

Equally important was asking myself the follow-up question: 'What am I going to do to feel that way?' This step is crucial because it connects intention with action. It's not enough to simply desire to feel good – you have to actively create opportunities for those feelings to manifest.

For example, if I wanted to feel grounded and centred, I might set aside time for meditation or take a walk in nature. If I wanted to feel creative and inspired, I'd schedule some time to work on a passion project or brainstorm new ideas. If I desired joy and connection, I'd prioritize quality time with loved ones or do something playful that lights me up.

This daily practice became my feel-good plan – a personalized roadmap for each day that helped me focus not only on what I wanted to achieve but, more importantly, on how I wanted to experience my day emotionally. It was a subtle but powerful shift that changed everything. Instead of just grinding through tasks, I was making deliberate choices that nourished my emotional well-being, ensuring that I wasn't just productive but also aligned with the core feelings that mattered most to me.

The beauty of this approach is that it empowers you to take control of your emotional state. You're no longer waiting for external circumstances to bring happiness, calm, or inspiration – you're actively creating those feelings for yourself, every single day. This exercise trains you to become more mindful of your emotions and more intentional about your choices, leading to a life that's not just busy, but deeply intentional.

### Steps
1. Every morning, ask yourself, 'How do I want to feel today?' and 'What am I going to do to feel that way?'

2.  Use a journal, like the one I created for myself called 'Reasons to Feel Good', to write down the feelings you want to cultivate and the specific actions that will help bring those feelings into your day.

3.  Make conscious choices each day to create the feelings you want.

**Outcome:** This daily practice helps you become more mindful about the actions you take, ensuring they align with how you want to feel, rather than just ticking off tasks for the sake of productivity.

# Visualization: The Power of Your Mind

Let's dive into another effective method to discover your future self: visualization. What is your vision for your life? Our minds are incredibly powerful. When we visualize something, our brain can't always distinguish between what's real and what's imagined. This is why visualization is such a potent tool for creating the future we desire. When we vividly imagine a scenario, we start to feel the emotions that come with it – whether it's joy, excitement, peace, or fulfilment. Those feelings, in turn, start to guide our actions and decisions, aligning us more closely with the reality we want to create.

Think about it: Have you ever imagined a worst-case scenario and felt real anxiety, even though it hadn't actually happened? That's because your brain and body react to what you're visualizing as if it's real. The same principle works in a positive way. When we visualize ourselves achieving something meaningful or living the life we truly want, we begin to feel the joy, excitement, and confidence that come with it. Those emotions fuel our motivation and actions, making our vision more likely to become reality.

By engaging in visualization, you're not just daydreaming; you're actively training your mind to align with your goals. It allows you to clarify your vision, strengthen your belief in what's possible, and build the emotional energy you need to bring that vision to life.

**Steps**

1. Reflect on the vision you had for yourself when you were younger. It might have been focused on a particular career, a dream home, or achieving certain milestones like starting a family or reaching financial independence.

2. Think about how your vision has evolved over time, as your circumstances and priorities have changed.

3. Consider what you currently envision for your future. What do you want now in terms of work, relationships, and personal fulfilment?

**Outcome:** This exercise will help you connect with how your vision for your future self is always evolving. As we grow, learn, and experience life, our vision of what success, happiness, or fulfilment looks like changes too.

# Journaling

Another wonderful way to explore your future self is by journaling about it. It allows you to take all the thoughts and ideas swirling in your mind and get them out onto a paper. This act of writing things down is like giving your brain a much-needed 'reset' – a brain dump that creates space for fresh insights and new perspectives.

The beauty of journaling is that it gives you the freedom to reflect without judgement. At first, you might write about your current thoughts or even the events of your day, but as you practice, it opens the door to something deeper. This is where stream-of-consciousness journaling comes in.

It's a technique about letting your thoughts flow freely onto the page, without worrying about grammar, structure, or whether it makes sense. You don't filter yourself; you simply write whatever comes to mind, even if it seems unrelated or random. This process taps into your subconscious, revealing feelings, desires, or fears that may have been hidden beneath the surface.

When it comes to envisioning your future self, journaling is a powerful way to explore your dreams, aspirations, and the person you want to become. By writing without constraints, you allow your true desires to emerge, helping you shape a vision that aligns with your core values and desired feelings. Grab a pen and paper, or open a blank document on your computer, and let your imagination run wild.

## Steps

1. Imagine yourself in a place that brings you immense joy and comfort. It could be sitting in a cozy cafe, by the beach, or anywhere that resonates with your heart. As you sit in this space, begin to imagine the life you've always dreamed of living. Picture yourself thriving – What are you doing? Who are you with? What does your life feel like? Let the details come alive in your mind, allowing yourself to fully embrace this vision.

2. Visualize someone you haven't seen in a long time approaching you and asking, 'How is life treating you? What have you been up to?' Imagine the warmth and curiosity in their voice as they genuinely want to know how your life has unfolded.

3. Explore the reasons why life is amazing for you. Dive deeper into what makes this imagined life so fulfilling – whether it's the deep connections you've built, meaningful relationships, personal accomplishments, or a profound sense of purpose and alignment. Reflect on how these elements contribute to your happiness and fulfilment.

4. Write freely in response, expressing the sheer amazement and fulfilment you feel in your imagined life. Let your words flow without judgement, capturing all the wonderful things you've experienced, the joy you feel, and the growth you've undergone. Focus on how your life aligns with the vision you created in Step 1.

**Outcome:** By journaling about your imagined conversation, you'll gain clarity and insight into the specific aspects of your ideal future that bring you immense joy and fulfilment. This process allows you to articulate and solidify your desires, creating a roadmap to manifest the life you envision.

By using these activities – identifying your desired feelings and creating a feel-good plan, visualization, and journaling – you'll get a clearer understanding of the path you want to take. They're not just exercises; they're tools to help you consciously shape the life you want to live.

# 4

# The Boat: Breaking Free from Survival Patterns

*Your worst enemy cannot harm you as much as your own unguarded thoughts.*

– Buddha

Now that we are clear about where you are in our current life circumstances and where we want to go next, the question arises: How do you get there?

The next phase of the journey answers that question. This path often feels difficult. The truth is, many of us are struggling, exhausted by all the effort we put in, only to feel like we're going in circles, making little progress. I call this part of the journey 'the boat'. For me, the boat represents how I had been navigating my life – constantly paddling against the current with a lot of effort, feeling exhausted, drained, and unsupported. Maybe you've felt this too.

The boat is that familiar place where we keep repeating the same struggles over and over, believing we need to work harder, do more, sacrifice more, and never stop in order to achieve our goals. The boat is a metaphor for the unnecessary but repetitive struggle we engage in when trying to reach the next phase of our lives, whether in personal or professional growth. This kind of struggle is a mindset we develop that tells us life has to be hard, that success requires self-sacrifice and pushing through exhaustion. This thinking held me back for many years – it holds many people back, and it's likely holding you back too.

When I rediscovered how I truly wanted to feel along the way – ease, creativity, nourishment, and freedom – it became obvious that my daily habits and behaviours were not aligned with those feelings. The boat, for me, was filled with things like complicated schedules, working non-stop on boring tasks, neglecting my health, not making any time to take care of my basic needs, much less anything else, and feeling trapped by the life I had created for myself.

I was doing the 'parent thing' where you starve yourself waiting to eat the inevitable leftovers from your children's plate – because who wants to waste food? I didn't feel good in my body as I wasn't exercising or stretching it. I spent almost all my time either sitting at a desk or driving my kids from one activity to the next. Every day looked and felt the same

- Wake up

- Make breakfast for the kids

- Caffeinate myself with a big cup of coffee

- Drop the kids to school

- Get to work and sit in back-to-back meetings

- Pick up the kids and drop them at their activities

- Head back to work

- Go home, cook dinner

- Frustratingly watch the kids eat at a snail's pace, waiting for those leftover scraps

- Do homework with the kids

- Engage in nightly debates and negotiations about bedtime

- Reward myself with a glass of wine and mindless TV

- Sleep

- Repeat

Although my routine was predictable, it clearly wasn't fulfilling. I was burning the candle at both ends, holding myself to unrealistic standards in all the roles I was playing – as a parent, a partner, and an entrepreneur. I convinced myself that this was just the way the real world operates, but the reality was that I had fallen into a routine of struggle.

I was on autopilot, and life didn't feel easy. It felt complicated and rushed, and I was exhausted all the time. I was clearly in survival mode, but I couldn't see a way out of that routine.

Sometimes we need a little help seeing things from a different perspective to catalyse change. That's exactly what happened to me when I was introduced to the works of Shirzad Chamine, Carol Dweck, Brené Brown, Eckhart Tolle, Louise Hay, and many others. There was a unifying message I gleaned from these works – our patterns of thought and behaviour are a result of past trauma or pain, but they don't have to define our future. Each of these thought leaders, in their own way, emphasized that transformation requires a change in thoughts, behaviours, and habits.

Our lives are made up of routines and habits that either serve us in a positive or negative way. If you aren't where you want to be in life, the likelihood is that you have some patterns and habits of thought and behaviour that are keeping you stuck where you are right now.

As I began to explore these patterns in my own life, I started to unravel the early childhood trauma and experiences that became unconscious protective mechanisms to keep me safe from emotional pain, rejection, and disappointment. These are essentially survival mechanisms, our mind's way of saying, 'I won't let this happen to me again.'

In my childhood, some traumatic events left me feeling like a victim and unworthy of love. My father, who I adored, pretty much abandoned my family when

I was eight years old, and not long after, my older brother, who was my hero, was killed. These moments made me feel like my world was completely out of my control. I started seeing myself as a victim of my circumstances, and I treated myself that way. I wanted people to feel sorry for me, and at the same time, I resented them when they did. It became a way for me to hide, to stay in the shadows, hoping for sympathy but rejecting it when it came.

Looking back, it was easier to lean into that victim mentality as it gave me permission to remain stuck. But there was another side of me that just wouldn't allow it. My natural drive and ambition started pushing me in the opposite direction. By the time I got to high school, I was overcompensating. I became an overachiever, constantly seeking attention and validation. I wanted to be everything and do it all. I joined clubs, not because I loved them but because I wanted to be seen as someone who could handle it all, as if collecting achievements would somehow erase the feelings of inadequacy I carried with me.

I remember writing out a list of things I needed to accomplish: captain of the volleyball team, form captain, acceptance into science subjects so I could one day enter medical school. Even though science didn't come naturally to me, I believed success could only look one way. I convinced myself that being a doctor was the ultimate achievement, even though literature and communication were the subjects that lit me up without even trying. I brushed off those passions because, in my mind, the only path to being successful was the one I'd decided on, whether I liked it or not.

I had built my entire identity around achieving those goals I had decided on, whether I liked it or not. When I didn't achieve them – when I failed the exams and couldn't keep up with the dream I'd built in my head – it felt like my entire world came crashing down. I didn't know what to do. My path to success had disappeared, and I was left wondering, what now?

Reflecting back to that time, I recognize the patterns that had been holding me back. These weren't just random failures – they were the result of deeper behaviours and beliefs I had developed over time. There are many terms used to describe these limiting behaviours – survival mechanisms, limiting beliefs, saboteurs, or self-protective patterns. Shirzad Chamine, author of *Positive Intelligence*, refers to them as 'saboteurs', mental habits that undermine our potential and happiness. Similarly, Mastin Kipp, a leader in trauma-informed personal development, speaks about how unresolved trauma creates 'survival patterns' that keep us stuck in cycles of fear and avoidance.

I personally prefer the term protective patterns because it suggests a sense of compassion and empathy towards ourselves. These behaviours aren't random or without purpose; they are strategies we adopted, often unconsciously, to shield ourselves from pain or trauma, especially those rooted in childhood.

These protective mechanisms helped us survive difficult situations by ensuring we avoided further harm or discomfort.

While necessary at the time, these protective patterns can start to hold us back once we're no longer in those environments. They become outdated survival strategies that operate in the background, limiting our ability to live fully.

These protective patterns helped us navigate those challenges and served an important purpose at the time. For example, we might have learned to avoid conflict, suppress our needs, or become perfectionists to gain approval or feel safe.

However, as we grow older and move out of those environments, these protective behaviours are no longer needed and begin to limit our potential and keep us stuck. For instance, the need to constantly please others or to avoid confrontation might have protected us from criticism or rejection in the past. But now, as adults, these behaviours can prevent us from setting boundaries or expressing our true selves. We think we're just living our lives, making decisions, or reacting to situations, but in reality, many of us are unknowingly operating on these old, protective patterns.

These patterns can keep us from experiencing the ease, joy, and fulfilment we genuinely desire because they're rooted in fear or avoidance rather than growth and authenticity. Recognizing and understanding these patterns is the first step towards healing and creating a life that feels aligned with who we truly are today – not who we had to be in the past.

This was a revelation for me. It really wasn't my fault that I was operating from an old survival strategy, but now that I was aware, I felt more empowered to do something about it. Knowing is half the battle, isn't it?

These survival mechanisms decided how I felt and how I acted. It's interesting how our early life experiences have the ability to shape our lives in ways that we don't even understand until much later on. Many of us don't make the connection between childhood trauma and our current life experiences – I certainly didn't.

I now understood how my thinking and behaviour influenced and kept me stuck in the survival life mode. This completely shifted my perspective, as I could now get to the root cause of the challenges I was facing. I finally understood why I felt the need to work harder, sacrifice more, and never say no – to feel worthy and loved. My protective patterns, driven by fear, guilt, and a need for approval, were in control. They kept me paddling upstream with endless effort, yet I never felt fulfilled.

The dominant pattern in my life was the deep-rooted belief that I wasn't enough. No matter what I did, I constantly felt like I didn't measure up. The childhood scars from my father and brother made me internalize the belief that I wasn't worthy of love. I convinced myself that people left because I wasn't lovable, which drove me to seek approval from others in the hope of feeling worthy.

This need for approval showed up in many ways, mostly in putting others' needs ahead of my own. I said yes when I wanted to say no, just to avoid disappointing someone or to feel helpful. But the result was resentment, sometimes anger, because I felt taken for granted. Whether or not that was true, I allowed my worth to be determined by others – and that wasn't their responsibility.

It became clearer to me how these thoughts were creating toxic behaviours in my life. The sense of unworthiness morphed into becoming an overachiever. It started in high school when I shifted from feeling sorry for myself to trying to be my best self – but that was just a guise for the scars. I was always striving to be the best at everything, thinking that if I could just be great at everything, then I'd finally feel like I was enough. I had convinced myself that I needed to work harder, be more, and do more to be lovable. I joined as many clubs as I could, strived for leadership positions, and wore as many badges as I could on my uniform to demonstrate my value. This is when my tendency to overcommit and burn the candle at both ends began, and it continued into adulthood. This was my way of shielding myself from the potential pain of feeling rejected and unworthy.

We all have ways we shield ourselves – whether by avoiding situations that cause us to feel anxious or snapping back when feeling threatened. Some of us choose to hide, pulling away from everyone. Others are on an endless hunt for approval, constantly seeking validation and reassurance from others.

These patterns shielded us, protected us, gave us something to cling to when times were rough. Yet, as we journey onward, there comes a point when we need to reassess. We need to ask, 'Are these patterns still my shield? Or have they become chains?' Do they pave a path for growth, or lead us through chaos and confusion?

Let's take a closer look at how some of these early experiences might manifest into protective mechanisms that, while they may have served us at one point, are now getting in the way of living our best lives.

## Protective Mechanism: Becoming Overly Self-reliant

### Trauma: Emotional Neglect

Perhaps you had parents who were less accommodating to your feelings and did not give you much empathy. You were not able to receive the love or reassurance needed, so you taught yourself to bottle up emotions and depend on yourself without expecting other people to step in. In adulthood, this may show up as hyper-independence. You become the one who requires no help whatsoever. However, being this way is exhausting and lonely. It prevents you from building real connections with others and from accepting support when you need it.

## *Protective Mechanism: The Trap of Perfectionism*

### Trauma: Parental Criticism or High Expectations

As a child, you may have been held to high expectations where good wasn't good enough. Perhaps your parents wouldn't accept anything less than the best from you, so you learned to equate your value with accomplishments. As a result, you work yourself to the bone, harder and harder to meet every target and be perfect. Sure, ambition and drive are great qualities, but are you happy? Likely not, because perfectionism is a moving target, and no matter how many times you accomplish something, it will never be enough.

## *Protective Mechanism: The People Pleaser*

### Trauma: Abandonment or Loss

You may have developed a fear of being left behind, whether in the form of a divorce, separation, or the death of a loved one. Longing for love and approval leads to trying to satisfy everyone else's needs. You say yes when you want to say no. You try your best to cover up feelings of anger or frustration to please and avoid abandonment. But what happens when you constantly neglect your own needs? You lose yourself in the process. That's the real loss of this protective behaviour – it stops you from showing up as your authentic self in both your personal and professional life.

## Protective Mechanism: The Guardian against Vulnerability

### Trauma: Physical or Emotional Abuse

When you grow up in an abusive environment, you learn to be on guard all the time. You're always waiting for the next hit or insult, either physically or emotionally. As an adult, you likely don't trust people, and you build walls around yourself to keep others out. You always expect the worst, and while that was useful as a child to protect you, as an adult, it prevents you from having healthy, trusting relationships.

## Protective Mechanism: The Need for Control

### Trauma: Erratic Care or an Unstable Environment

If you grew up in an unpredictable environment where you had little stability and felt powerless, that could manifest as a need to control everything in adulthood. You may find yourself needing order and structure in your space and relationships to avoid powerlessness. This need for control can manifest in obsessiveness, creating predictability to the point where spontaneity and learning from others are stifled.

## Protective Mechanism: Avoiding Rejection
### Trauma: Bullying or Social Disapproval

If you felt rejected or bullied in childhood, this could manifest as a tendency to avoid situations that might expose you to rejection. You may distance yourself from social settings, stay in the background at work, avoid speaking up, or keep yourself busy to avoid feeling vulnerable. This mechanism keeps you playing small and prevents you from stepping into your full potential, both personally and professionally.

## Protective Mechanism: Hyper-vigilance and Anxiety
### Trauma: Witnessing Domestic Violence

Growing up in a home where violence was a constant threat creates hyper-vigilance. You're always scanning your environment for danger. Even as an adult, this anxiety can carry over, leading you to expect the worst even in secure environments. It's often difficult to let down your guard and relax, constantly feeling that something is about to go wrong, which takes a toll on both your psychological and physical well-being.

## Protective Mechanism: Becoming the Fixer
### Trauma: Taking on Adult Responsibilities as a Child

Children of dysfunctional homes, such as those with an alcoholic parent, are often forced to grow up too quickly, taking on adult responsibilities like caring for younger siblings or even their own parents. These children grow up to be adults who tend to 'fix' other people's problems. It becomes second nature, leading to toxic relationships in both personal and professional life. They seek out people to 'fix' and eventually feel resentful because their needs are not being met.

## Protective Mechanism: The Scarcity Mindset

### Trauma: Financial Instability

If you grew up in an environment where money was tight, you're likely to develop a scarcity mindset, believing there is never enough – even when you have enough. This mindset may lead to hoarding, shying away from financial risks, or becoming a workaholic to ensure you're never in that position again. The scarcity mindset isn't limited to money; it can also apply to relationships, time, and opportunities, ultimately harming your well-being.

No matter the reason, these protective mechanisms eventually turn against us. They keep us in a kind of survival mode, making it difficult to move towards the life we desire, both personally and professionally. Recognition and awareness of these patterns is the first step in freeing ourselves.

Change isn't easy. These old habits fight back. When I took on the role of CEO at the Branson Centre of Entrepreneurship, those feelings of not being enough, those old patterns, those same doubts, and old fears returned – 'Am I enough?' Every challenge was viewed through the lens of those beliefs. I believed I wasn't smart enough, I wasn't strong enough, and I needed to learn more. I was waiting for someone to find out that I wasn't right for the job – Imposter Syndrome set in.

The global pandemic didn't help, as I was now coping with homeschooling my children and making tough decisions at work while my mental and physical well-being was compromised. Then came that day when it all became too overwhelming, and I found myself curled up under my desk at home, tears streaming down my face, feeling the weight of the world.

My son found me there, bringing me back to many years earlier when I had just started my entrepreneurial journey, paralyzed by stress. I'd been here before and knew the signposts. It was time, once again, to find my compass, take those deep breaths, and remember who I was beyond the challenges.

I tell you this story because I want you to know it's okay not to get it right all the time. We are not perfect, and this is a part of the process. You may feel like you're regressing, but it's quite the opposite – you're learning and growing through the many phases and spirals of life.

This phase was to get me off the boat that had been steering my path for far too long. At that moment under the table, I realized I had fallen back into survival mode. The difference this time was that I knew how to get back out. My friend and mentor showed me I could rewrite my story about my past trauma and choose to take responsibility for my feelings, thoughts, and actions. My heart, mind, and actions didn't have to be prisoners of the past. To heal and change, I had to stop blaming others or circumstances. I had to face my beliefs and thought patterns to overcome them. It was on me. So I chose. I chose to think differently, to feel differently, to act differently.

What patterns have been showing up in your life? In what ways have you been protecting that inner child who doesn't want to be hurt again?

I encourage you to take the time to look at your own patterns of behaviour. This part of the process is critical to move forward. Without doing this work, which can bring up old hurts and pains, you'll be left in the loop of your current challenges, just like I was when I found myself under that table crying. Getting to the root cause of your behaviour is the only way to make the shift; otherwise, you're just putting a sticking plaster on the issue.

Can you identify with any of the protective patterns listed in the next section? How have these patterns shown up in your life?

# Protective Patterns

- **Self-sacrifice Syndrome**

  This pattern drives you to prioritize everyone else's needs above your own, leaving you feeling depleted and unappreciated. It stems from a desire to feel needed and valued, but it often leads to burnout because you rarely take time to nurture yourself. The belief that taking care of yourself is selfish keeps you stuck in a cycle of constant giving.

- **The Fixer Trap**

The Fixer Trap compels you to take responsibility for others' problems, believing that their success or happiness depends on your intervention. It can lead to micromanaging and feeling anxious when things don't go as planned. This desire for control stems from a need to feel secure, but it can create tension and strain in your relationships.

- **The Perfectionist's Prison**

This pattern makes you believe that if things aren't perfect, they aren't good enough. It drives you to set impossibly high standards for yourself and others, often resulting in feelings of frustration and disappointment. The Perfectionist's Prison keeps you trapped, constantly striving for flawlessness, which prevents you from embracing progress and celebrating your efforts.

- **Hiding in the Shadows**

Hiding in the Shadows is when you hold back from sharing your true potential, fearing judgement or failure. You might downplay your talents or avoid taking risks because it feels safer to stay in your comfort zone. This pattern often comes from a fear of standing out or being seen, which keeps you from stepping into your full power.

- **Catastrophe Mindset**

The Catastrophe Mindset expects the worst in every situation, causing constant anxiety and tension. It keeps you on high alert, preparing for scenarios that might never happen. This pattern can make even minor setbacks feel like major crises, preventing you from fully enjoying the present and seeing the positive possibilities around you.

- **Disconnecting from Inner Guidance**

This pattern emerges when you second-guess your intuition and inner voice, doubting the guidance that comes from within. Instead of trusting yourself, you seek answers externally or rely heavily on logic, which can leave you feeling disconnected and uncertain about your path. It stems from a fear of making the 'wrong' choice, but it limits your ability to act confidently.

- **Numbing Out**

Numbing Out involves using external substances or behaviours – like food, social media, alcohol, or other habits – to escape uncomfortable emotions or stress. It's a way of avoiding the deeper issues you don't want to confront. While it may provide temporary relief, it keeps you from truly addressing the root causes of your discomfort and finding more sustainable ways to cope.

- **Avoidance Loop**

  This pattern involves putting off tasks or decisions, especially those that feel overwhelming or uncomfortable. It's a protective mechanism that seeks to avoid failure or discomfort, but it often results in more stress and guilt as deadlines loom closer. The Avoidance Loop keeps you stuck in a cycle of inaction, preventing you from achieving your goals.

- **Staying Stuck**

  Staying Stuck keeps you in relationships – romantic, professional, or social – that drain you and hinder your growth. This pattern can come from a fear of being alone, a sense of obligation, or a belief that things will get better. It prevents you from setting boundaries and seeking connections that nourish and uplift you.

- **Validation Seeker**

  The Validation Seeker is constantly looking for external validation to feel worthy and accepted. It can lead you to change your behaviour, suppress your needs, or conform to what others expect, even when it doesn't align with your true self. This pattern stems from a fear of rejection and keeps you from embracing your authenticity.

· **The Clarity Block**

The Clarity Block shows up when you avoid making decisions by claiming confusion. It's a way of protecting yourself from the responsibility or potential consequences of a choice. While it might feel safer to stay in uncertainty, this pattern keeps you from moving forward and taking ownership of your path.

## *Journal Activity: Uncovering Your Protective Patterns*

Before diving into the deeper work of shifting your mindset, it's important to first uncover the protective patterns or self-sabotaging behaviours that may be holding you back. These patterns often stem from old survival mechanisms and limiting beliefs. If you're unsure of what these patterns might be, I highly recommend taking an assessment to help identify them. One assessment I found particularly useful is Shirzad Chamine's 'Positive Intelligence Saboteurs' assessment, which you can find in the resource section at the back of this book.

Once you've done that, the following journal prompts will help you explore the root causes of these patterns. Set aside some quiet time to reflect and write without overthinking. Let your subconscious mind guide the process, allowing the insights to flow naturally.

## Journal Prompts

- Which protective patterns do you think show up in your life? Which one feels dominant?

- Can you remember a time when this pattern first appeared in your life? What triggered it?

- What behaviours do you default to when you feel uncomfortable or threatened?

- When have you held yourself back out of fear?

- What stories do you tell yourself about yourself?

- How do the stories others tell about you affect your self-perception? Do you accept their version of who you are, allowing their interpretation to shape your reality?

By working through these questions, you'll begin to uncover the layers of your protective patterns and gain a deeper understanding of how they influence your thoughts and actions.

# Taking Control: Becoming the Captain of Your Ship

Once you identify your protective patterns, the next step is learning how to shift from this struggle mindset. The answer is simple: you've got to get off the boat and become the captain of your own ship! While getting out of the boat won't be easy, I know you're ready to take on this challenge. It's going to feel tough at times, but it will be worth it.

In the next chapter, I'll share how I learned to take control of my journey, and to reprogram my brain to serve me better during life's challenges. Together, we'll navigate how to leave the old patterns behind and embrace a new way of thinking and living.

# 5

# The Ship: Navigating Life with Purpose and Well-being

*Your life is your ship, and you are the captain. Sail it with purpose, courage, and joy.*

– Michael Josephson

Congratulations! You've hopped off the boat, and now it's time to board the ship. By now, you've explored the foundations of your journey:

- **Island A:** Your current life mode, where you've gained clarity on whether you're in survival, stability, success, or significance mode.

- **Island B:** The vision of your future self, based not on rigid goals but on the feelings you desire to experience.

- **The Boat:** A metaphor for the protective mechanisms and limiting patterns that have kept you in place, often steering you away from what you truly want.

Now it's time to explore what life on the ship looks like. The ship is where we navigate with purpose, intention, and a focus on leading a more balanced, joyful life. If the boat was about surviving, the ship is about thriving – moving through life with more ease and clarity. It's about shifting from reactive survival patterns to proactive, conscious living.

You might be thinking, 'This sounds great, but how do I actually make this shift? After all, it's easier said than done to change years of ingrained habits and limiting behaviours.' I get it. When I first began this journey, I didn't realize how much my mindset was shaped by outdated beliefs about success and self-worth. I thought I had to push harder, work longer, and achieve more to feel good about myself. But true transformation isn't about exhausting yourself – it's about creating a way of living that sustains both your personal and professional growth.

# Shifting from Survival to Thriving

Moving from the boat to the ship means letting go of old patterns and learning to navigate life with new tools. It's about recognizing that success isn't just measured by external achievements but by how well we navigate the process. Life rarely goes according to plan, and that's okay. With the right tools and mindset, you'll learn to adapt and manage life's unpredictability with more resilience and grace.

This chapter marks the transition into exploring the three key pillars that will guide you along the way: self-care, self-awareness, and creating value. Together, these pillars will serve as your foundation for flourishing in every aspect of your life. But before diving into them, it's important to understand why this shift is so crucial.

When I reflect on my own journey, I realize that the most important relationship I had to nurture was the one with myself. Prioritizing my well-being was no longer just a personal decision; it became the foundation for how I could excel in every area of life, including work. This shift wasn't about striving for success at any cost – it was about creating a sustainable strategy that allowed me to succeed without burning out.

## *The Pillars of the Ship*

Think of the ship as a metaphor for your journey towards your future self. Like any vessel, the ship needs three key elements to operate:

- **An anchor** to keep you grounded.

- **A compass** to guide you in the right direction.

- **Sails** to catch the wind and move you forward.

These three elements are mirrored in the three pillars of this framework: **self-care**, **self-awareness**, and **service** (see Figure 3). Each pillar provides the tools and strategies needed to keep you aligned, balanced, and moving forward in the right direction.

- **Self-care** serves as your anchor, ensuring you remain steady even when life's seas are rough.

- **Self-awareness** acts as your compass, giving you clarity on who you are and where you want to go.

- **Service** provides your sails, helping you move towards your goals by contributing meaningfully to something beyond yourself.

As we delve into these pillars, you'll see how this framework supports not only your personal growth but also how it strengthens your ability to lead, innovate, and succeed. In a world that often prioritizes productivity over well-being, this approach offers a way to create lasting success without compromising your health or happiness.

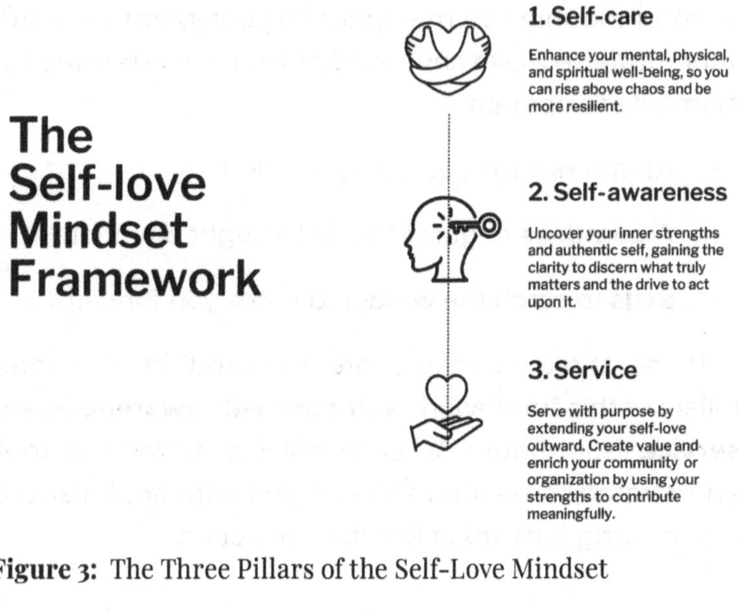

## The Self-love Mindset Framework

### 1. Self-care

Enhance your mental, physical, and spiritual well-being, so you can rise above chaos and be more resilient.

### 2. Self-awareness

Uncover your inner strengths and authentic self, gaining the clarity to discern what truly matters and the drive to act upon it.

### 3. Service

Serve with purpose by extending your self-love outward. Create value and enrich your community or organization by using your strengths to contribute meaningfully.

**Figure 3:** The Three Pillars of the Self-Love Mindset

# Pillar 1

# Love Yourself

*You yourself, as much as anybody in the entire universe, deserve your love and affection.*

— Buddha

This pillar guided me out of survival mode and into a place of stability.

I had just had my first child when I decided to quit my corporate job to pursue my dream of being my own boss. I envisioned working from anywhere and enjoying all the free time I would have to spend with my new baby. Except, I had no time.

I had created a more stressful job for myself, with longer hours and less pay. My nights were spent writing proposals, my days fulfilling client work and seeking new business. Everything I had hoped for now felt like a pipe dream. The more the business grew, the further I drifted from the person I wanted to be and the life I wanted to have.

I was snapping at my family, spending less time with my children (yes, I now had a second child), doing work I no longer enjoyed, and resenting my clients. The work no longer felt good, and my motivation and drive dwindled with each passing day. I knew something was wrong when I was happy to lose a client.

I continued to ignore all the signs, numbing myself with a nightly glass of wine or a tub of ice cream. But the stress became too much for me to numb anymore. The reality of entrepreneurship, coupled with the challenges of being a parent to a baby and a toddler (team no sleep), spun me into a spiral of anxiety, frustration, depression, and eventual burnout.

One day, I sat in my living room feeling sorry for myself because I felt like I was failing in every part of my life

- as a mother,

- as a partner, and

- as an entrepreneur.

I felt helpless, trapped, and completely defeated. I couldn't breathe. I literally couldn't get up.

That's the reality of burnout – you reach a point where you simply can't go any further. Burnout happens when stress goes unaddressed for too long. I had ignored every sign: the racing heart, constant fatigue, headaches, and emotional numbness. I wasn't taking care of my physical, mental, or emotional needs. I was burning the candle at both ends, hoping everything would resolve itself.

But the problem with that mindset is that it never ends. If you keep ignoring your well-being, your body and mind will only continue to break down.

As I sat there, I suddenly remembered being a little girl and my mother collapsing at work. She had blacked out from an anxiety attack caused by chronic stress. I remembered how she later told me how terrified she was – not just for herself but for us kids – afraid of not being around for us.

I realized that the same thing was happening to me.

I cried. I screamed.

Then, in that moment, I made a decision. I committed to no longer blaming people, circumstances, or my ambition for what was happening to me.

I had to make a choice, and I knew I wanted something different for myself. My children needed a better version of me, and I wanted to feel like myself again – or at least some calmer, happier version of me. Truth be told, at that point, I just wanted to function as a human being again.

I had to stop everything. The business came to a screeching halt because I had to take care of myself. That's the thing about stress, fatigue, and anxiety – you think you are managing until it knocks you over and leaves you with nothing more to give.

I stopped chasing clients, stopped pursuing all the projects swirling in my head, and let go of the need to check everything off my to-do list. I focused on doing the bare minimum and scaled back my workload. It wasn't ideal, especially as an entrepreneur. I couldn't just take a vacation or call in sick – I had to work if I wanted to get paid. But none of that mattered because I knew that if I didn't address what was happening to me right then, things would only get worse.

Just giving myself permission to stop trying to solve every problem brought me a small moment of relief. That one moment led to another, and then another. It was a wake-up call. If I couldn't take care of myself, how could I effectively run a business and a team? How could I make clear, strategic decisions to grow the business when I was running on fumes?

That was when I recognized that personal well-being is not separate from professional success – it is the foundation of it. I had to learn to prioritize myself and take responsibility for my health in a way I hadn't before.

I went on my healing journey to rest, renew, and reconnect with myself. At first, the change was uncomfortable as I had to break those old habits that had been ingrained in me for so long. But I started small: a morning walk, a commitment to eight hours of sleep, saying no to things that drained my energy.

Gradually, I noticed the impact. It was exactly what I needed to start feeling like I could breathe again without my heart pounding in my chest. I noticed a change not only in my body but in my work. I was clearer, more focused, and able to approach challenges with renewed energy.

Self-care became a way of life for me.

I dived deep into learning healing modalities to help bring my mind, body, and soul back into alignment. What do I mean by that? Alignment is when your thoughts, feelings, and actions are working in harmony. You'll know when you have that alignment because you'll feel at ease. You won't doubt yourself or seek validation from others. You will be decisive and confident.

When I was in the throes of burnout, I felt pulled in so many directions. My mind was constantly racing with thoughts of what I should be doing, my body was weak, my heart was palpitating, and I felt confused and disconnected from the work I was doing.

I found wellness and self-care tools to navigate that chaos and confusion. That's when I learned about the power of self-love through self-care. I was so focused on achieving and being successful that I gave everything to the business – my time, my energy, my love – leaving nothing for myself, let alone for the people who mattered most to me.

When you love yourself, you make your well-being a priority. When you make your well-being a priority, you strengthen yourself – mind, body, and soul. When you have a strong mind-body-soul connection, you can better manage and navigate the inevitable challenges of life.

One thing I learned on this journey is that you can't escape challenges – they are part of life and growth – but you don't have to struggle through them.

That's the difference.

Self-care is a holistic approach that considers all aspects of your well-being: mind, body, and soul. This approach is neither prescriptive nor a one-size-fits-all philosophy. It's very much a personalized and unique approach for each individual. As you go through this section of this book, take what resonates with you. I'm sharing techniques that worked for me and may work for you too. In some cases, the principle is universal, but the modality will depend on you. For example, the idea that movement is beneficial for your body is the principle, and the modality could be swimming for you and kickboxing for me. If you read the next few chapters through that lens, you'll benefit greatly from these concepts.

At first, I didn't realize how transformative holistic self-care could be. Like so many others, I had grown accustomed to neglecting my well-being and was stuck in bad habits that prevented me from exploring what would truly nourish me. Change is uncomfortable because when we are pushed outside our comfort zones, our brain responds by protecting us from what it perceives as dangerous. The danger is anything new and unfamiliar.

If you try to stop drinking coffee cold turkey, your body reacts with a massive headache because it's used to functioning with caffeine. However, the longer you go without it, you'll notice that you feel better once your body adapts.

When your body is used to being sedentary, sitting all day, and you start to exercise, your body responds with aches and pains.

If you aren't used to sitting still in meditation, it feels like a mammoth task to manage your restlessness.

All of these examples demonstrate that we default to our old programming and patterns because they are habits. They are what we are accustomed to doing.

Starting this journey requires willpower and a commitment to break those habits. But guess what? You'll be okay. You aren't in any danger, and you are the captain of this ship, deciding how far you're willing to go. Of course, that's easier said than done. For that reason, I'm going to share some of the tools, techniques, and concepts that have helped me along my self-care journey.

This pillar is the fundamental first step to creating an anchor in your life that can support you in becoming more resilient in challenging times and propel you forward during times of ease. When you take care of yourself, you create the internal conditions necessary for growth. We'll explore this first pillar, starting with the mind, as I believe every transformation begins with the power of thought.

# What Does It Mean to Care for Yourself?

Caring for yourself is about creating a strong foundation for your overall well-being and personal growth. It involves treating yourself with kindness, patience, and understanding, recognizing that you are deserving of the same care and attention you give to others. It's about listening to your needs – physical, emotional, and mental – and give yourself permission to rest, recharge, and prioritize your needs.

## *Why Does It Matter?*

Before prioritizing self-care, you may have been living in a constant state of stress, burnout, or chaos, reacting to life's demands without a strong foundation for your well-being. Shifting your focus to care for your well-being changes this. When you prioritize your mental, physical, and emotional health, you build resilience and strength to navigate life's challenges and make more intentional choices.

# Benefits of Prioritizing Your Well-being

1. **Increased energy:** By nurturing your mind, body, and spirit, you feel more energized and alive. Feeling good physically and mentally motivates you to continue practising self-care.

2. **Stronger self-trust:** When you trust yourself, you let go of doubt and are confident in your decisions. You know that no matter the outcome, you'll learn and grow from it.

3. **Healthier relationships:** When you're secure in yourself, you no longer rely on others for validation or to fill emotional gaps. You bring your best self into relationships, allowing for more balanced and fulfilling connections.

4. **Boost in confidence and motivation:** Caring for yourself helps you become your own advocate and cheerleader. You see your potential, give yourself patience and grace, and take meaningful action towards achieving your goals.

# How to Start Prioritizing Yourself

We'll explore this journey through three key areas:

1. **Mind:** Overcoming limiting beliefs and habits by building mental strength.

2. **Body:** Listening to your body and using nourishing practices to maintain health.

3. **Soul:** Reconnecting with your inner self and reigniting your desires.

In the following chapters, we'll dive deeper into each of these areas. By taking care of yourself in these ways, you'll find more balance and the strength to rise above life's challenges with confidence and ease.

# 6

# **Nurture Your Mind: Mental Well-being and Mindset**

*We cannot solve our problems with the same thinking we used when we created them.*

– Albert Einstein

Our minds are powerful tools that can either propel us towards greatness or, if left unchecked, hold us back, making us feel like we're stuck in a cycle of self-sabotage. My mind used to sabotage me all the time. To be honest, it still does. But now, I have the awareness to recognize when it's happening and can stop my thoughts from spiralling too far downward into a cycle of destruction.

One of the most profound moments in my life tested this awareness. My son, Sebastian, had always struggled with asthma, so when he started having trouble breathing, I initially thought it was just another asthma flare-up. I was feeding him soup when I noticed something wasn't right. His breathing was laboured, and his chest was rising and falling rapidly. As someone who had grown up with asthma, I recognized the signs and immediately sprang into action. I used all the techniques I had learned over the years – his inhaler, positioning him upright, calming him down – but nothing worked. His breathing kept getting worse.

The fear began to rise in my chest, but I stayed focused, thinking I just needed to get him to the accident and emergency department. I grabbed him and rushed out of the house, driving as fast as I could to the nearest hospital. My heart was racing as I tried to reassure him, but inside, I was terrified. I kept glancing at him in the rear-view mirror, watching him struggle for breath, and I felt utterly helpless.

When we arrived at the first hospital, they turned us away. They said they didn't deal with paediatric cases, and because it was during the COVID-19 pandemic, there were strict regulations about whom they could admit. The rejection felt like a punch to the gut. My child couldn't breathe, and no one was willing to help. Panic threatened to consume me, but I didn't have time to break down. I scooped him up and ran back to the car, my mind racing as I headed to the next hospital, one that specialized in children.

As I drove, Sebastian's voice broke the silence. 'Mommy', he said, his voice weak and strained, if I die, I love you.

Those words shattered me, but I couldn't let him see that. Everything inside me wanted to scream, to cry, to panic, but I knew I had to stay strong for him. I swallowed my fear and replied, 'You're not going to die, baby. You're going to be okay.' I didn't know how I kept my voice steady, but I did. Deep down, I knew I had to stay calm for both of us.

When we finally reached the children's hospital, it felt like an eternity before a doctor could see him. My nerves were frayed, but I continued to hold it together. He was given round after round of treatment with the nebulizer, and nothing seemed to work. I watched my son, his small body exhausted, and my heart broke. The doctors were concerned it could be a severe complication from COVID-19, and they mentioned isolation and the possibility of it being something fatal. Hearing that word – fatal – was like the ground dropping out from beneath me.

At that moment, everything I had learned about reprogramming my mind clicked into place. This was the true test. I remembered a story about how we can never really know in the moment whether something is 'good' or 'bad'. We often rush to label situations as one or the other, but the truth is, we don't know what's unfolding. What seems like the worst moment of our lives might be leading us to something greater, or what appears to be an unbearable obstacle could teach us our most important lesson.

I didn't know what was going to happen. I had no control over the medical situation. But I did have control over my mind. I could spiral into fear and let anxiety consume me, or I could choose to refocus my thoughts on a positive outcome, on strength, and on the belief that my son would be okay. I chose the latter.

I walked him into the isolation room with a calm mind. It wasn't easy, but I knew I had to focus on what I could control – my energy, my thoughts, and how I showed up for him. Every minute felt like an hour, but I kept reminding myself to stay present, to take it one moment at a time, and to hold on to the belief that everything would turn out okay.

Over the next few days, I tapped into every mindset technique I had ever learned. I shifted my focus whenever fear crept in, redirected my thoughts, and practised grounding exercises to keep myself calm. It wasn't just for me – it was for my son. I knew that he needed to feel my strength so that he could find his own.

After several tests, it turned out that he had pneumonia. It wasn't the deadly side effect of COVID-19 that the doctors had feared. After a few rounds of antibiotics, his breathing improved, and he was back to his normal, energetic self. The relief was overwhelming, but so was the realization of how much my mindset had helped me through those terrifying days.

This experience cemented everything I had been practising about reprogramming the mind. I have no doubt that if I hadn't built my mental muscles – if I hadn't trained my brain to stop spiralling into worst-case scenarios – I would have fallen apart during that time. But instead, I was able to stay grounded, resilient, and present for my son when he needed me the most.

This was the most impactful test of the training I had done. It wasn't about denying the fear – it was about facing it with a different mindset, one that allowed me to rise above the chaos and stay in control of my thoughts. That, in turn, allowed me to stay strong for my son, and together, we made it through what could have been one of the darkest periods of our lives.

This experience was a powerful reminder that our thoughts have immense power, especially in the face of crisis. If I hadn't trained my mind to focus on strength and resilience, the fear could have overwhelmed me.

This was the exact mindset I had to call upon again in my professional life. Although the situations were different, the mental and emotional challenges were surprisingly similar. Just like when my son was sick, I faced uncertainty, fear, and self-doubt. Just as I had chosen to rise above fear for my son, I had to make the same choice for myself in my professional life.

As I stepped into this new role of leadership, I experienced waves of self-doubt. I questioned my abilities, compared myself to others in similar positions, and feared judgement from my peers. But I knew that if I let those negative thoughts take root, they would hold me back. I had learned from the experience with my son that my mind could either be my greatest ally or my worst enemy. I had already seen the power of a reprogrammed mind in action, and I knew that I could apply the same tools to my professional journey.

When I first took on the role of CEO, I compared myself to others in similar roles, always believing they had something I lacked. In fact, after getting the job, I half-expected to receive a call telling me they had made a mistake. Surely, they would see I wasn't suited for the role. I believed I wasn't good enough, didn't know enough, and often felt like an imposter beneath the confidence I portrayed.

My mind was anchored in past experiences where I felt hurt by others' opinions of me. I was constantly in a state of trying to validate my worth, and here I was doing it again. Except this time, I realized I was the one doing it to myself. The anxiety I was experiencing in this new role was very familiar. My heart was racing, I was indecisive, and I struggled with sleep. I knew all the signs of stress because I had been here before. I knew I needed a mindset shift.

Though I'm not a psychologist, I have navigated self-doubt, unhelpful beliefs, and the stress that comes with them. This chapter isn't theoretical; it's practical. It's based on real-life strategies, tools, and techniques that transformed my life and leadership, helping me to reprogram my mind to serve me better during challenging times.

Remember the boat analogy on Island B from earlier? The one where we're stuck, paddling tirelessly against the current but not getting anywhere because of habits and protective patterns of behaviour? One of my dominant protective patterns was hiding in the shadows. I was so scared of being judged or failing that I avoided taking any risks.

Before joining the Branson Centre, I worked at a similar organization, and when the opportunity to apply for the CEO position came up, I went for it. I was confident that I could do the job, having worked closely with the then-CEO, who had become a mentor to me. Together, we ran the organization, and I was trusted to make strategic decisions. I learned the ins and outs of the role and felt prepared to take the lead. However, when the time came, naysayers surfaced. People told me I wasn't qualified enough, I wasn't visible enough, and, worst of all, I couldn't balance leadership with being a new mom.

One colleague even said, 'No one believes you can do the things you say you're going to do.' I remember being so shocked by that comment – I wasn't sure why they would even think that way. I had been contributing, making decisions, and delivering results, so hearing those words felt like a punch to the gut.

At the time, I had just had my second child. I was still breastfeeding, and every evening, instead of staying late to socialize, attend events, or connect over drinks like others in the industry, I rushed home to nurse my baby. I remember feeling torn between wanting to be present at these networking events and the more pressing need to care for my newborn. It seemed like no one understood the juggling act I was managing – balancing the demands of a new baby and a growing career. Because I couldn't always stay late or attend every event, I started to feel like I was being left out or overlooked. The informal social gatherings where deals were discussed and connections were made became moments I missed, and I soon noticed I wasn't invited as much anymore.

Those doubts planted by others started to take root. I began questioning myself, feeling rejected, and retreating into the shadows. My mind latched onto their criticisms, replaying every comment until they became my own beliefs. I withdrew, no longer confident in my abilities, and I let their doubts seep into my sense of self-worth.

That's why the idea of becoming the CEO of the Branson Centre felt so terrifying. It wasn't just a new role – it was another opportunity to be judged. The success or failure of the organization would rest on my shoulders, and I couldn't help but wonder, What would those same naysayers think of me now? Would they still believe I wasn't enough?

Reflecting on this, I realized just how much mental energy I had wasted on other people's opinions of me. I had spent years letting their doubts cloud my vision, but the truth is, they probably weren't even thinking about me anymore. They had their own lives to live, their own battles to fight, and their own successes to celebrate. Even if they were still thinking about me – What did it matter?

I came to understand that courage was what I needed to reprogram my mind. I had to stop letting the voices of doubt run my narrative. If I was going to step fully into my role at the Branson Centre, I needed to break free from those negative patterns of thought and fully embrace the leader I knew I could be.

So, how can we rise above these self-protective patterns and reprogram our minds to better serve us?

It all starts with our thoughts. Negative thoughts tend to snowball, dragging us into a downward spiral of negative emotions. Fortunately, the same mechanism applies to positive thoughts, but negative thoughts are often more pervasive. They attach themselves to other negative thoughts, triggering behaviours that become habits that don't serve us.

Science has shown that our thoughts create patterns in our brains. When certain thoughts are repeated, synapses in our brain fire together, forming connections that strengthen over time. This is how thoughts become beliefs. A belief is just a thought you keep thinking, and those beliefs are the basis of our protective patterns. If you keep telling yourself that putting others first is a sign of being a good person, then that belief starts to inform your behaviour.

For example, if a colleague at work is curt with you one day, your mind may spiral with thoughts that this person doesn't like you. Your brain then searches for evidence to support those thoughts, ultimately leading you to change your behaviour with this person, trying hard to win their approval – all because of that initial assumption, which may not even be true.

Our brains are wired for survival because our ancestors had to constantly face and overcome the dangers of the natural world. As a result, our brains look for ways to conserve energy in case of a fight-or-flight scenario. The brain tries to be as efficient as possible, finding shortcuts that allow us to navigate the world without expending too much mental effort.

Those shortcuts become our habits. Habits are ways of thinking and behaving that become second nature through practice and repetition. For example, if you drive and realize you got home without thinking about the route, you've experienced this kind of mental efficiency. It's as though the car knows its way home. Your mind and body are on autopilot, following a pathway the brain has created without conscious effort.

These patterns of thought and behaviour are often linked to our protective patterns. A people-pleaser, driven by the fear of rejection, might view a colleague's curt behaviour as a sign they are not liked. This can lead to seeking validation and constantly trying to win approval. A perfectionist may react to any perceived criticism by being overly self-critical, convincing themselves they need to work harder to avoid failure. In both cases, these negative behaviours stem from a series of thoughts rooted in perceived threats that keep us stuck in habits that limit our growth.

Identifying my own protective patterns was an important first step. Once I could identify the negative behaviour, I could name it, and become more aware of its presence in the moment.

# Becoming Aware of Your Thoughts

To interrupt this negative spiral, you first have to become aware of these negative thoughts. We have thousands of thoughts a day, most of which we aren't even aware of. However, we experience our thoughts through physical and emotional sensations like a racing heart before speaking in front of a crowd or a sense of heaviness when feeling overwhelmed.

The next time you feel anxious, stop and ask yourself:

- What is my body telling me?

- What thought am I thinking that has triggered this feeling of anxiety?

- Is that thought true? Or is this my protective pattern speaking?

When you do this, you give yourself a moment of pause to assess what's really going on before the thought starts to build momentum. When a negative thought has built enough momentum, it's hard to stop it. Like a train moving at top speed, you can't just slam the brakes and change direction; you have to slow down, come to a complete stop, and then move in the opposite direction. When you practice becoming aware of your thoughts before they build momentum, it becomes easier to choose more useful thoughts.

It all boils down to this:

Our thoughts create emotions, emotions influence our actions, and actions repeated over time become habits. Reprogramming your mind means understanding how these are all connected and changing the patterns that shape your life.

Take some time to reflect on these connections and consider how they manifest in your own experiences. It's through this awareness that we can begin to untangle and transform these patterns, paving the way for personal growth.

# Steps to Reprogram the Mind

Let's break it down into simple steps:

### Step 1: Become aware of your physical body and notice the cues it's giving you

It's useful to keep a journal and observe what's happening when you feel various emotions. I began to notice what my body felt like when I experienced emotions such as anger, happiness, sadness, being overwhelmed, anxiety, worry, excitement, and eagerness. For example

- **Anger:** My body heats up, starting from my feet up to my head. My heart pounds, my breathing shortens, and I feel very impatient.

- **Joy:** My body feels tingly and beaming with light. I smile a lot and become very patient.

- **Anxiety:** My heart pounds, it feels like I can't breathe, I feel confused, and I can't sit still.

- **Overwhelm:** My head hurts, my body feels tired, and I just want to sleep. I procrastinate.

- **Happiness:** My breathing is calm and regulated, so much so that I don't even notice it. I feel neutral and content in my body, with little brain chatter. I'm mindful, observing small things around me.

Once I became aware of what I was feeling, I could pause in the moment to assess what thoughts were swirling in my head.

## Step 2: Distract your brain

Becoming aware of a thought doesn't stop it from building momentum. Just like the train analogy, you can't just go in the opposite direction without first coming to a stop. Consider this distraction to be like pressing the reset button. One of the most effective ways to refocus your brain away from negative thoughts is by engaging your senses – touch, sight, sound, smell, and taste. Engage with your surroundings by touching something, noticing scents, observing your environment, and listening for specific sounds.

These exercises are helpful when you are spiralling and can be done anytime, anywhere. Try it.

- **Touch:** Feel the surface of something nearby, like a desk, a piece of clothing, or even your own skin. Notice what it feels like. Is it rough, smooth, hard, or soft? Does it have texture? Spend time doing this, and your thoughts will shift towards noticing what you're physically touching.

- **Sight:** Look at something close by or in the distance and notice it in intricate detail. Describe how the light or darkness hits it. What colour is it? What texture does it have? What material is it made of?

- **Sound:** Listen for something nearby or in the distance. What can you hear? How many sounds are there? Can you identify where they are coming from?

- **Smell:** What can you smell? Notice the scent of your coffee or the food you're about to eat. You could also carry something with you, like an essential oil, to smell when you need calm or energy. I use an essential oil diffuser in my office and carry a small bottle of oil in my purse to help me stay calm when I feel anxious.

- **Taste:** Tasting something intentionally – whether it's sipping tea or coffee, savouring the flavours in your mouth, or enjoying a piece of chocolate or any meal mindfully – can help you pause and focus.

Once you have an awareness of your thoughts, the key is to catch them early and redirect your mind's focus. The brain can only focus on one thing at a time, so by engaging your senses, you can divert attention from negative thoughts. When you're caught in a negative thought spiral, it's difficult to immediately transition to positive thoughts. By pausing and using distraction, you can gradually shift to more useful thoughts.

Try incorporating two or more of these senses. I use these exercises regularly, both to manage negative emotions and amplify positive ones. The more you practice training your brain to focus on command, the stronger your ability to reprogram your mind becomes, and the less time it takes to shift from negative thoughts to useful ones.

## Step 3: After this distraction, choose a better-feeling thought

By consciously engaging your senses, you create a pause in the negative thought patterns and redirect your mind towards more positive experiences. This is not about denying or suppressing negative thoughts, but giving yourself a moment to regain balance and shift focus to more empowering thoughts.

To break free from these thought patterns, we need to step outside our comfort zones and face our fears. Our greatest strengths are often found on the other side of fear – I know this for sure.

When you become aware of a pattern, take a step in the opposite direction of your usual behaviour. For example, if you're used to always putting others first and neglecting yourself, prioritizing your own needs will likely feel uncomfortable at first.

Breaking these patterns and setting new boundaries may cause resistance, both within yourself and from others. People might feel uneasy or upset with the changes. But this is a natural part of the process. After reinforcing old habits for so long, it's only normal for going against them to feel like a struggle.

You might feel like you're doing something wrong.

It feels like a part of you is fading away because, in a sense, it is. Those old patterns that held you back are being challenged. It might feel intense, as though a part of you is dying. But as I discovered, the discomfort eventually subsides. You realize people can manage without your immediate attention. The more you commit to breaking your patterns and establishing boundaries, the easier it becomes to align with your true self and function at your best.

It's important to embrace the discomfort and recognize that it's necessary for growth. The initial struggle is just your outdated programming exiting. You're still here, stronger than ever, and your inner wisdom is about to shine even brighter.

A crucial first step in self-care is reprogramming your thinking, but that's not the end of the story. The body and mind are intertwined – having a healthy body has a major impact on keeping your mind healthy, and vice versa. Proper nourishment of your body supports your mental, emotional, and physical health.

Neglecting your physical health can have the same consequences as negative thought patterns: preventing you from reaching your full potential and leaving you feeling anxious, ill, exhausted, trapped, and uncomfortable. The mind–body connection is real, and both must be cared for.

Chapter 7 examines how intentionally nourishing your body is a vital step on your journey towards becoming the best version of yourself.

# 7

# Nourish Your Body:
# Physical Health
# as Self-care

---

*The greatest wealth is health.*

— Virgil

I realized that success isn't just a mental game – it's a physical one too. When I began to nourish my body with the right foods, movement, and rest, I found myself more energized, focused, and ready to handle the challenges of life and business. Proper nourishment wasn't just about fuelling my body; it became fuel for my career as well.

I remember the day I committed one year of my life to learning about health coaching. I didn't initially set out on this journey to transform the lives of others – I did it for myself. I was tired of my own excuses and ready to feel better in my body. After having my two children, I held onto the extra weight long after they were old enough to talk and even crack jokes about it. I had tried many methods to lose weight – most of which left me feeling deprived and stressed. But when I found this health coaching programme, it was like someone had given me the keys to a door I had been trying to open for years. It took me a while, but I soon learned how to do more than just feed my body; I learned how to genuinely nourish it.

It was no longer about losing weight; it was about listening to what my body needed to function at its best. Instead of telling my body that I hated it by depriving it, I began fuelling it with food, movement, and a renewed sense of compassion for myself.

Make no mistake, neither this understanding nor my transformation happened overnight. Overcoming the fear of being judged by others, and mostly my own self-criticism, required a great deal of mental effort. As we discussed in the previous chapter, I had to face and overcome long-standing behaviours that had been my crutch for years. I made excuses about not having time to exercise; I ate my feelings – and trust me, I had plenty of those. I had that nightly glass of wine to drown out the world and all its worries. These practices became habits that I needed to shake, but as I worked through the mindset changes, I needed a lot of self-compassion.

Self-compassion is showing yourself kindness and respect during times of struggle. It requires acknowledgement of the self-protecting patterns, the trauma you've experienced, and the current challenges you face. You will go through many emotions as you make these shifts in your life, but reminding yourself to be compassionate and knowing that you are on a journey of transformation will make all the difference. It's what I had to do on a daily basis when I didn't like how I felt in my clothes or what I saw in the mirror. I decided to change the narrative and thank my body for everything it had done for me. I would literally thank every part of my body for keeping me alive and functioning. This practice allowed me to build more self-compassion. As I acknowledged the miracle that is my body, I began to love it more, and loving it more meant I wanted to take better care of it. So, how did I do this?

# Food as Fuel

I started by educating myself on how food could actually support my well-being. I learned that eating whole, unprocessed food made me feel significantly better. I began cooking more meals for myself and my family instead of ordering in or eating out. Following the philosophy I learned in my health coaching programme, I focused on adding more nutritious options rather than eliminating foods from my diet. This approach helped me transition without feeling deprived or experiencing withdrawal.

I gradually incorporated more fruits and vegetables into my meals, and over time, this naturally pushed out most of the processed and sugary foods. By prioritizing whole, unprocessed ingredients, my palate began to shift. I found myself enjoying foods that truly nourished me, rather than just filling me up.

Here is where taking 100% responsibility for your own well-being comes into play again. It's a choice you make every day. I used to make excuses about being too busy with work meetings and kids' schedules. I would run from one meeting to the next fuelled by caffeine. The result was feeling ravenous by the end of the day and eating anything in sight, which left me consuming calories that offered no nutritional value.

It took being intentional with my planning, but here's what I did:

- Packed nutritious snacks like nuts, dates, and dark chocolate in my bag for work.

- Meal prepped food that could be used throughout the week and carried lunch with me to work.

- Listened to my body and how it responded to specific foods. There is no one-size-fits-all. You have to know what's going on with your body to make the right choices for yourself.

This became even more evident to me when my daughter, who had been struggling for years with food, was finally diagnosed with coeliac disease. Her body can't process gluten, which destroys her intestines and makes it difficult for her body to absorb nutrients. Since she was a baby, we thought she was a picky eater and just small for her age. I thought I was giving her a well-balanced diet, but it turns out her needs were different from mine. All this to say, no one can tell you the exact diet you should follow – you have to find out for yourself. My daughter never liked sandwiches or anything with flour, but I didn't know it was making her sick. In hindsight, I regret telling her to eat up or getting annoyed that she didn't finish her food. She was listening to her body, but I wasn't listening to her. Similarly, we don't listen to ourselves.

When you get bloated after eating something, your body is trying to tell you something is wrong. Don't ignore it. When you get headaches from eating citrus or chocolate, don't ignore it. You have alternatives that can satisfy you without suffering. We aren't taught to listen to our bodies when they tell us they're full. Some of us believe we have to finish what is on the plate and treat our bodies like garbage receptacles. I used to do that with my children's leftovers. I didn't want to see the food go to waste, so I put it into my body, allowing my temple to become a receptacle for my kids' trash. That's completely unacceptable to me now. If my body is full, I need to listen. As you go on this journey of loving your body, make time to get to know it.

A great technique is to journal about how food makes you feel. It can be a quick note you jot down to record your findings. You'll soon be able to incorporate more of what makes you feel good.

# Movement

Exercise is an important part of your health and well-being. For me, this meant taking an active role in my physical fitness. I discovered yoga around this time, and it was nothing short of transformative. While it deeply enriched my spiritual journey, it also became a medium for me to reconnect with my body. This practice paved the way for other physical activities – kickboxing, badminton, tennis, brisk walks, and just being intentional about my physical well-being became part of my daily routine.

I looked for movements that I enjoyed instead of feeling like it was punishment. I strongly believe you need to find something that makes you feel good and brings you joy. Start with something fun – maybe it's a sport or dancing. It doesn't have to be the gym or a traditional approach.

I didn't stop there. I looked for fun ways to make movement a natural part of my daily life. One of my favourites is taking regular dance breaks, where I listen to my body's intuition and let loose. Dancing has become a key part of my routine, and I even have impromptu dance parties with my kids. It's how I wake them up in the morning – it's fun for me, though they're usually a bit grouchy! But deep down, I know they love it. The point is, you can find unique ways to incorporate movement into your everyday life.

# Hydration

One of the simplest yet most impactful habits you can adopt for your overall well-being is staying hydrated. It's something many of us overlook, especially when we're busy or relying on caffeine to get through the day, as I once did. I used to reach for coffee or other caffeinated drinks, thinking they would give me the boost of energy I needed to power through. But what I didn't realize was that I was chronically dehydrated, and that dehydration was actually contributing to my fatigue.

Sometimes our bodies send signals of dehydration that we misinterpret as hunger, which led me to overeat when all I really needed was water. It was a surprising realization when I learned that the brain's signals for thirst are often mistaken for hunger, and as a result, I found myself reaching for snacks when what my body truly craved was hydration.

Hydration plays a crucial role in your mental and physical health. When your brain and body are properly hydrated, everything functions more smoothly. Your concentration improves, your energy levels rise, and your mood stabilizes. It's amazing how something as simple as drinking more water can dramatically affect your mental clarity, helping you feel more focused and less sluggish throughout the day.

There are countless reasons to stay hydrated. Water regulates your body's temperature, delivers essential nutrients to your cells, lubricates your joints, aids digestion, flushes out toxins, and keeps your skin looking radiant. Every system in your body relies on water to function properly, yet studies show that most adults don't drink nearly enough water to stay adequately hydrated.

I realized that I wasn't giving my body what it needed to thrive, and once I started to prioritize hydration, I saw massive improvements in my overall well-being. My energy levels increased, I felt more alert, and even my digestion and skin improved. It made me wonder why I hadn't been paying more attention to something so simple all along.

If drinking plain water doesn't appeal to you, there are many ways to get creative with hydration. Infusing your water with fruits like lemon, berries, or cucumber can make it more enjoyable, and it's a great way to boost your vitamin intake at the same time. Herbal teas are another excellent option, especially those with hydrating herbs like mint or hibiscus. You can also eat foods with high water content, such as watermelons, cucumbers, and oranges, to supplement your hydration.

Remember, staying hydrated is a small daily habit that can make a big difference in how you feel, think, and perform. It's a foundational step towards taking care of your body, and once you get into the habit, you'll notice how much better you feel when you give your body the hydration it needs.

# Rest

Without adequate sleep, it's impossible to perform at your best. Our bodies and minds need time to repair and recharge, and sleep is a fundamental part of that process. Sleep impacts every area of our lives – personal and professional – and neglecting it can have profound negative effects. I've experienced this first-hand, and

I know how much of a struggle it is to show up fully when I'm sleep-deprived. That's why making sleep a priority is essential for me.

Arianna Huffington, in her book *Thrive*, describes a similar realization. She recalls a moment when her lack of sleep led to her collapsing from exhaustion. That experience became a wake-up call for her about the importance of sleep in achieving well-being and success. Her story resonated with me because I, too, have seen how lack of sleep affects not only my productivity but also my mood, clarity, and overall ability to function.

Over time, I've learned that it's not just about getting seven to eight hours of sleep – it's about quality sleep and finding what works for me personally. For me, it's about allowing my circadian rhythm and natural sleep cycles to align with my lifestyle. This means making intentional choices to create a sleep routine that supports my rest and renewal.

One of the most important steps in my sleep routine is turning off digital devices at least an hour before bed. The blue light from screens can disrupt melatonin production, which is essential for falling asleep naturally. Instead of scrolling on my phone or watching TV, I've found that reading a few pages of a book helps me wind down.

I also use a diffuser with calming essential oils like lavender, which has been shown to promote relaxation and improve sleep quality. Adding magnesium lotion to my nightly routine has also made a difference – magnesium helps with muscle relaxation and eases tension, preparing my body for rest. Another key part of my routine is drinking a calming and healthy tea that soothes my body and mind before bed.

Creating these rituals helps signal to my body that it's time to rest. It's all about finding what works for you, but for me, it's about tuning in to my natural cycles, aligning with my body's rhythms, and taking a holistic approach to rest. By prioritizing sleep, I not only improve my personal well-being but also set myself up for success in my professional life.

We all have periods of high energy when we feel alive, productive, and sociable – these are the moments to embrace and maximize our output. But when our energy dips, it's important to listen to our bodies and take the time to rest. Slowing down isn't a sign of weakness; it's a necessary part of the cycle that allows us to speed up when the time is right. By honouring these natural rhythms, we can show up more fully in every area of our lives.

# Deepening the Commitment to Physical Care

My journey into self-care and physical fitness took another pivotal turn when I decided to be proactive about my health. It was time to replace fear and ignorance with knowledge and action. I committed to regular check-ups with my physician. It wasn't just about catching potential issues early but also about understanding my body better. I set annual check-ups to understand better what was happening with my body. I wasn't willing to live in the dark anymore. By taking this step, I equipped myself with information, empowering myself in the process.

I dived into the world of vitamins, minerals, and herbs. While the Internet is flooded with generic advice, I made it my mission to tailor this knowledge to my own unique needs. I educated myself about what specific nutrients my body required and which natural supplements could enhance my overall well-being. This wasn't about following trends; it was about carving a health path that was distinctly mine.

Taking care of my physical self had a ripple effect on my professional life. When I was physically fit and well-nourished, I found that I was sharper, more focused, and could handle stress more effectively. I also showed up with more confidence when I felt good on the inside and outside.

# Personal Style

How you present yourself to the world matters. I realize that how I show up tells people how I expect to be treated. Style is how you express yourself and one way to communicate who you are to the world. It matters that you be intentional with how you want to show up. You get to choose. There is no right or wrong way. It's your way. Wear clothes that express your style, make you feel comfortable and confident.

When I was in university, I loved style and fashion, and I showed up feeling good wherever I went because my outsides reflected what I felt on the inside – confident, beautiful, and bold. When I became a mother, I gained almost 60 pounds during both of my pregnancies, and the weight stuck around even after the babies were out of nappies. I didn't feel good in my body, and I was ashamed of it. At the time, I didn't have much self-compassion to remind myself that this was a natural part of the process, so I decided to do nothing about it. I made excuses that I didn't have time to take care of myself because I had more important things to do, like taking care of my children. Of course, I now know that this was just a manifestation of my martyr and survival mode.

My journey of physical self-love also revolved around tiny yet significant acts. Whether it was splurging on my favourite tea (yes, just for me and not the entire household) or indulging in an epsom salt foot bath after a long day, I was learning to prioritize myself. As a parent, it's easy to slip into patterns of self-neglect. I decided to change that narrative. Instead of nibbling on my kids' leftovers, I started making warm, delicious meals tailored just for me. Because why shouldn't I enjoy something beautiful and nourishing? Additionally, I made it a point to truly relish my meals – no emails, no distractions. Just me and my plate, in a moment of mindfulness.

# Crafting Your Personalized Well-being Plan

Diving into the world of well-being can feel overwhelming. But here's what I've learned: while there's no magic formula, carving out a plan for your body's nourishment that speaks to your heart, your rhythms, and your life's demands is the secret sauce. Think of this action plan as a series of questions to help you draft your very own well-being story. It's about digging deep, finding what lights you up, and ensuring that each step you take resonates with you personally. So, take a deep breath, grab a pen, and let's co-create a nourishment journey that feels authentically you.

Taking baby steps with even a handful of these pointers can spark a genuine transformation in your physical health, spilling over into heightened focus and clarity in your work life. Always bear in mind: it's about keeping the rhythm, not going all out at once. It's those small, consistent habits that create beautiful, enduring wellness.

- **Start small:** If you're new to exercise or haven't been active for a while, it's essential to start slow to avoid injury. Begin with 10-minute sessions of light exercises and gradually increase the duration as your stamina improves.

- **Schedule workout time:** Block out specific times in your calendar for physical activity, just as you would for a meeting. Prioritize this time and make it non-negotiable.

- **Desk exercises:** Incorporate simple stretches or exercises you can do at your desk or during short breaks. Chair squats, seated leg lifts, or even desk push-ups can be effective.

- **Walking meetings:** Instead of sitting in a conference room, propose a walking meeting. This can be refreshing and spark creativity.

- **Take the stairs:** Whenever possible, opt for stairs instead of the elevator. It's a quick way to get your heart rate up and strengthen your legs.

- **Stay hydrated:** Keep a water bottle at your desk. Staying hydrated not only benefits your health but can also improve concentration.

- **Meal preparation:** Dedicate a few hours each weekend to preparing healthy meals for the week. This ensures you always have a nutritious option on hand, reducing the temptation of fast food or unhealthy snacks.

- **Invest in ergonomics:** Consider ergonomic office furniture or standing desks. This can prevent posture-related issues and encourage movement.

- **Set alarms:** Use your phone or computer to set reminders to stand, stretch, or take a short walk every hour.

- **Join a gym or class:** Many gyms offer classes before or after standard work hours, catering to working professionals. Find a routine that fits your schedule.

- **Educate yourself:** Make an effort to understand the nutrients, vitamins, and minerals essential for your body. Seek advice from nutritionists or health coaches if necessary.

- **Routine check-ups:** Regularly visit your physician for check-ups, ensuring that any potential issues are identified early.

- **Mindfulness and breathing:** Incorporate short mindfulness or deep-breathing sessions into your day. While this nurtures mental well-being, it also positively impacts your physical state by reducing stress.

- **Prioritize sleep:** Ensure you're getting adequate rest. Sleep plays a vital role in physical recovery and overall health.

- **Join a fitness group:** Engaging in group activities like cycling clubs, running groups, or even dance classes can provide both social interaction and physical benefits.

As a leader, I knew it was important to lead by example. Well-being isn't just for my benefit – it's a message to my team that health and wellness are a priority in our company culture. To truly embody this belief, I expanded this mindset across the company, encouraging everyone to make time for their own personal well-being journey. I wanted the team to know that they had the space and freedom to prioritize their health and personal lives, just as I had learned to do.

One of the ways I implemented this was by introducing a four-day workweek, giving everyone a longer weekend to recharge and balance work with personal commitments. In addition, we adopted a remote or hybrid work model where team members could work from anywhere – whether that was from the office, their home, or even the beach. The only condition was that the results needed to be there, but I wanted them to have the flexibility to work in a way that suited their natural rhythm.

For some on the team, this approach was life-changing. There were those who had health challenges, family matters, or children to take care of, and this freedom allowed them to attend to those things without the pressure of rigid office hours. They could structure their day in a way that worked best for them, leading to improved performance and engagement. I noticed that, with these changes, team morale skyrocketed. People were happier, more energized, and more focused.

Through these initiatives, the team also began to realize just how important self-care truly is. When they had the time and space to take care of their physical, emotional, and mental health, their productivity increased, and the quality of their work improved. It reinforced a key lesson: when people are empowered to take care of themselves, they bring their best selves to work.

This shift led to us adopting a more people-centred leadership approach. We embraced the ethos of our founder, who always believed that if you take care of your people, they will take care of the business. I am a testament to the fact that this is absolutely true. Our team's well-being became central to our company's success, proving that when you prioritize health and happiness, everything else – productivity, creativity, engagement – naturally follows.

In retrospect, this holistic approach to physical care – be it through doctor visits, personalized nutrition, or exercise – has been one of the most rewarding investments I have ever made. Not just for the personal satisfaction it brings, but for the tangible impact it has had on my professional life. When my body is nourished and well-cared for, my mind is sharper, my energy levels are higher, and I'm able to tackle challenges with a clearer, more focused outlook. It has become clear to me that taking care of your body is not a luxury; it is an absolute necessity for every sphere of your life. Whether you're leading a business, managing a team, or balancing the demands of family and work, your physical well-being forms the foundation for it all.

More than anything, caring for my physical self has been about aligning my body with the life I want to lead. It's not just about being fit or looking good – it's about honouring the temple that houses my soul, acknowledging its needs, and giving it the respect it truly deserves. Our bodies are incredible vessels that allow us to pursue our dreams, nurture relationships, and experience the fullness of life. Without health, everything else becomes secondary. By making my well-being a priority, I've learned that the better I treat myself, the more I can give to my work, my family, and the world around me.

So, as you go through your own journey, remember that the time and care you invest in your body isn't selfish or indulgent – it's an essential part of living a fulfilling, balanced life. Your body is your foundation, and when you prioritize its care, everything else in your life has the potential to thrive.

# 8

# Connect with Your Soul: Following Your Desires and Inner Guide

*When you feel powerless, it's because you stopped listening to your own heart. That's where power comes from.*

– Gianna Crow

Caring for and strengthening my mental and physical fitness were essential aspects of my self-care journey, allowing me to love myself in a way I hadn't before. However, I soon realized that this wasn't enough – I needed to nurture my soul connection too – that inner flame that's much bigger than just my physical body.

This concept is often overlooked in the professional world, where we focus on goals and external achievements, rarely making time to connect with our inner selves. Yet, the truth is, we are guided by this inner self in every aspect of our lives. In this final chapter on self-care, we will explore how connecting with that deeper part of ourselves can serve as a trusted voice – one that knows our true desires.

When I talk about the inner self, I'm referring to that inner knowing, that inner guidance system – your intuition. This isn't about religion or spirituality, but rather about tuning into a deeper part of yourself that knows what you truly desire and need. We've all experienced moments when we've said, 'I went with my gut feeling' or 'I trusted my gut.' That's your inner flame speaking.

However, the more we neglect our mind and body, the more susceptible we become to stress, exhaustion, and burnout. This disconnection makes it harder to tap into our intuition. We can't think clearly, and we're not in a calm state to hear when our inner voice is speaking. This is especially evident when we lack confidence. Confidence is trust in yourself. When you trust yourself, you don't seek external validation.

As children, we had a strong connection to our inner desires. We would dress however we wanted, without a care for others' opinions, confidently expressing ourselves. But over time, we stopped listening to those desires, and instead, we began conforming to fit in. We wanted to avoid judgement and criticism, so we silenced that inner voice. Trusting and listening to your inner voice goes against conformity.

For example, setting boundaries is an act of listening to your inner self. It's about saying yes to what aligns with your desires and no to what doesn't. When you have strong boundaries, you don't bend easily. In my professional life, I was once told that having strong boundaries was one of my weaknesses in advancing my career. But I wasn't willing to compromise on my time with my family. It was a non-negotiable for me to be the one picking up my kids from school and hearing about their day, instead of sitting in a weekly meeting.

I remember even further back, right after returning from maternity leave, my manager gave me advice that went something like this: 'To truly excel in your role, you need to get a live-in nanny and stay late at work.' In other words, to move up the ladder, I had to sacrifice time with my child to prove my dedication to the company. Needless to say, I quit soon after, and that decision marked the beginning of my entrepreneurial journey. Listening to my intuition back then was the best decision I ever made.

Now, I'm not suggesting that you leave your job because someone says something you don't want to hear, but my intuition was so strong, guiding me towards something bigger. It wasn't easy, and I made many mistakes along the way. But that decision led me from being an employee in a middle-management role to becoming the head of an organization that allows me to bring my whole self to work. I now have the time and space to be the best mother I can be while making a global impact through my work. Had I not followed my intuition, I would likely still be in an environment that wasn't right for me, stuck on the hamster wheel.

Your inner voice communicates through your desires – the things that excite you and light you up. These desires should not be ignored. There's a reason you have those longings in your heart, and it takes courage to listen to them. However, that courage is eventually replaced with confidence and certainty when you live by following your desires.

# Ways to Connect with Your Inner Self

Connecting with your inner self is about tuning in to the wisdom that already resides within you. In the midst of life's chaos and demands, it's easy to lose touch with that deeper part of ourselves, the part that knows what we need, what we want, and how to guide us forward. Often, we seek answers outside ourselves, but the truth is, the answers are already within us. The key is learning how to listen.

The following activities are designed to help you reconnect with your inner self and create space for the clarity, peace, and guidance you need. Each one serves as a tool to quiet external noise, align with your true desires, and foster a deeper relationship with yourself. Whether it's through journaling, meditation, practicing gratitude, or spending time in nature, these practices allow you to rediscover who you are and what truly matters to you.

By making time to engage in these activities regularly, you cultivate a stronger sense of self-awareness and a deeper understanding of what your heart and soul are trying to tell you. Let's explore how these practices can help you on your journey to greater self-connection.

## *Journal about Your Desires*

Writing down your desires, big or small, is a powerful exercise in self-discovery. Often, we suppress our deepest wishes due to fear, doubt, or a belief that they aren't realistic. Journaling about your desires gives you the space to explore your heart's truest longings without judgement or restrictions. This isn't about practicality; it's about letting yourself dream without limits. By putting your desires on paper, you allow them to take shape, transforming abstract thoughts into something tangible. This practice can be liberating because it gives your dreams a voice, opening up the possibility for action.

The benefit of this technique is that it helps you clarify what you truly want, even if it's something you haven't yet acknowledged. Once your desires are clear, you can start to break them down into actionable steps. No matter how big or far-fetched the dream seems, every goal starts with small, manageable steps. This approach makes even your wildest dreams feel achievable, as you focus on what you can do today to get closer to what you want.

## *Meditation*

Meditation is a transformative practice that helps you connect with your inner self, a space where clarity and peace reside. On my own journey, meditation became a cornerstone of how I learned to listen to my inner voice. It's a practice that quiets the noise of the outside world and the distractions of your mind, allowing you to hear the wisdom that always exists within. When you meditate, you strengthen the muscle of inner awareness, helping you tap into answers that are already inside you.

Meditation has numerous benefits, including reducing stress, increasing focus, and improving emotional health. For me, meditation became not just a practice of stillness, but a tool for problem-solving. Whether it's sitting in silence for 10 minutes each morning or engaging in guided meditations, the practice helps you hear what your heart is telling you. Asking yourself, 'What does my heart want me to know today?' during meditation is a simple yet profound exercise that can lead to powerful revelations about your desires, intentions, and next steps.

## *Gratitude*

Practising gratitude has a way of grounding you in the present moment and shifting your focus from what you lack to what you already have. It's easy to get caught up in desires, goals, and future aspirations, but gratitude keeps you anchored in the here and now. When you regularly reflect on what you're grateful for, you create a mindset of abundance, which opens you up to even more good things in life. This shift in perspective can improve your mood, reduce stress, and create a sense of fulfilment, no matter where you are on your journey.

The benefits of gratitude are both emotional and psychological. By acknowledging even the smallest joys – whether it's a warm cup of tea or the kindness of a friend – you train your brain to focus on positivity. Starting and ending your day with gratitude helps you remain mindful of the good in your life, fostering a sense of contentment and joy. It also reinforces a mindset that attracts more of what you're thankful for, leading to a virtuous cycle of positive thinking.

## Nature

Spending time in nature is a deeply restorative practice that reconnects you to the earth and, ultimately, to yourself. Nature has a unique way of slowing you down, quieting your mind, and bringing you into the present moment. Whether you're walking through a forest, sitting by the ocean, or simply spending time in a park, nature grounds you in a way that everyday life often doesn't allow.

The benefits of being in nature are vast – studies show that time spent outdoors reduces stress, boosts creativity, and enhances overall well-being. For me, being in nature is one of the easiest ways to reconnect with my intuition. When I feel overwhelmed or disconnected from myself, a simple walk outside can clear my mind and bring me back to centre. The sounds of birds, the rustling of trees, or the warmth of the sun on my skin remind me of the simplicity of life, and in that stillness, I find answers. Nature provides the perfect backdrop for reflecting on your desires, listening to your inner voice, and feeling a sense of calm that makes space for clarity.

Incorporating these techniques – journaling, meditation, gratitude, and time in nature – into your life can profoundly affect how you connect with yourself, helping you tap into your desires and align with your true path. Each of these practices provides different benefits, but they all serve the same purpose: to help you reconnect with your soul and listen to what it's telling you.

# Leaning into the Seasons of Your Life

Listening to your inner voice involves understanding that we all have seasons in our lives. Just as nature cycles through spring, summer, autumn, and winter, we experience our own cycles of change and transformation. These seasons are essential to our growth, providing us with opportunities to nurture, reflect, and evolve. Embracing these natural rhythms allows us to live more authentically and find balance in every stage of life.

An essential part of nourishing your soul is recognizing the season you are currently in. There are times when we need to be more gentle with ourselves; other times, we feel the urge to socialize and shine brightly. Sometimes we crave solitude for quiet reflection, or we might be bursting with energy and enthusiasm. Acknowledging these shifts allows us to honour our true desires and needs, rather than forcing ourselves to conform to external expectations or routines that no longer serve us.

This realization was a crucial part of connecting with my inner flame. Have you ever established a routine, gained momentum, and then one day fell off track? Perhaps you started to feel guilty for missing days at the gym or not sticking to your plan. In those moments, it's important to practice self-compassion and listen to your intuition. Ask yourself whether it's your default protective patterns showing up – like perfectionism or fear of failure – or if it's your inner voice expressing a genuine desire for rest and rejuvenation, connection with others, creativity, or a period of observation.

The beauty of recognizing your life's seasons lies in their uniqueness. Each one holds profound lessons and serves a particular purpose, much like the seasons in nature. Here's how I see them unfold:

### Spring: A Time of Renewal and New Beginnings

Spring represents the season of new growth, energy, and renewal. It's when we plant the seeds of new ideas, relationships, and ventures. In this phase, life feels fresh with possibility. There's a sense of excitement in the air, much like the sprouting of flowers after a long winter.

For me, spring often came at pivotal moments when I embarked on a new project, like the first steps into entrepreneurship or welcoming motherhood. It was a time of hope and possibility, where creativity flowed, and the future seemed full of potential. But just like in nature, spring also requires nurturing. The seeds we plant – whether they are new habits, relationships, or business ventures – need our attention, care, and patience to grow. It's a time for taking action but also for being mindful of what we're investing our energy in.

**Summer: A Time of Flourishing and Abundance**

Summer is when the seeds planted in spring come to fruition. It's the season of abundance, where the hard work we've put in begins to pay off. Life feels vibrant and full; we feel energized and ready to share our gifts with the world. During summer, we often find ourselves in the flow, thriving, and making the most of the opportunities that come our way.

In my life, summer represented the seasons when everything seemed to align – my role as the CEO of the Branson Centre, for instance, was one of those times. It was a period of flourishing professionally and personally, where I felt deeply connected to my purpose and able to lead with clarity. But summer can also bring its own challenges, such as the temptation to overextend ourselves. It's easy to get caught up in the busyness of success, forgetting to pause and reflect on what truly matters. This season is about celebration, but it also requires balance – making time for both the outer world of achievements and the inner world of reflection.

## Autumn: A Time of Reflection and Harvest

Autumn symbolizes harvest and letting go. It's a time of gathering the fruits of our labour, reflecting on what worked, and acknowledging what didn't. It's also the season of transition, as the leaves fall and nature prepares for the coming winter. In our lives, autumn may appear as a time when we feel the need to release what no longer serves us – whether it's outdated beliefs, unfulfilling relationships, or old habits.

For me, autumn represented moments of introspection and change. There were times when I needed to step back and evaluate my path – like when I experienced burnout, trying to juggle multiple roles as a mom and business owner. I had to let go of certain expectations and ideas I held about success. Autumn teaches us the importance of release, creating space for what's to come. It's also a time for gratitude, appreciating the wisdom we've gained from the experiences we've cultivated.

## Winter: A Time of Rest and Inner Growth

Winter is the season of rest, stillness, and introspection. Just as nature retreats and conserves energy in the colder months, so do we. This season may bring feelings of stagnation or uncertainty, but it's also a time of deep internal growth. It's a period for slowing down, tuning into our inner voice, and nurturing ourselves in ways that may not be outwardly visible.

Winter has shown up in my life during periods of transition, like when I faced emotional and physical exhaustion from constantly giving to others while neglecting myself. It was during these moments of quiet that I discovered the importance of self-care and reflection. Winter teaches us patience and the power of stillness. It's a reminder that growth doesn't always happen on the surface – sometimes the most profound changes take place in the quiet spaces of our lives.

In these winter moments, I found clarity and inner strength, understanding that rest is not a sign of weakness but a vital part of regeneration. I began to see that, just like in nature, we need periods of dormancy to restore our energy and prepare for the next phase of growth.

By tuning into your inner voice and honouring the season you're in, you can discern what you truly need. Trusting your intuition helps you make choices that align with your authentic self, rather than forcing yourself to adhere to rigid expectations. Embracing these natural cycles allows for personal growth and a deeper connection with your true desires.

When you recognize the seasons in your life, you start to honour the flow of life itself. Each season has its gifts: spring brings renewal, summer celebrates abundance, autumn offers wisdom through reflection, and winter provides space for rest and deep personal growth.

By embracing where you are in the present moment, you'll not only find peace with the ebb and flow of life but also align more closely with your inner truth, allowing you to navigate life with grace, self-compassion, and purpose

# Cultivating Your Inner Voice: A Daily Practice

Making time to connect with your inner voice is crucial. Just as building mental and physical fitness takes time, learning to listen to and trust your inner voice is a process. It won't happen overnight, but with consistent effort, you can cultivate this connection and let it guide you in your life – both professionally and personally. In today's busy world, carving out time for this practice is essential. It doesn't have to be first thing in the morning, but I've found that early mornings are ideal because you haven't yet been bombarded by the demands of the day. Bob Carter's saying resonates deeply with me: 'Poor planning on your part does not constitute an emergency on my part.'

How often have you found yourself moving to the beat of someone else's drum? You wake up, check your emails and messages, and suddenly your day is hijacked by someone else's to-do list. This used to be my reality. I would start my mornings by diving into emails, setting my priorities based on what others delegated to me. While some of those tasks were important, I realized that I was always reacting to others' demands instead of focusing on my own. What if, instead, I set the tone for my day based on my inner desires?

Now, instead of jumping straight into social media or emails, I prioritize connecting with my inner self. I take a moment to ask myself: What do I want to feel today? How can I align my actions with my inner desires? This simple shift allows my day to flow from a place of intention rather than reaction.

When we don't honour our own desires and neglect to build that soulful connection, we end up in reactive mode, constantly responding to external stimuli. This can lead to frustration and resentment. I used to feel as though my day had been hijacked by other people's moods, requests, and complaints. I'd wake up, check my email, and frantically respond, which set off a chain reaction of being in constant response mode. By the end of the day, I felt drained, out of control, and frustrated because it felt like someone else was steering my life.

To establish boundaries, you must take a proactive approach to your life. When you tap into your inner desires, you gain clarity about what truly matters to you, and that clarity helps you create and maintain boundaries. You'll stick to these boundaries because you understand the 'why' behind them. This also leads to better planning in all areas of life – both personal and professional. When you stand firm in your priorities, others begin to respect your boundaries.

I remember a friend in the corporate world who had strong boundaries around her time. Once she pulled into her driveway, our conversation would end because that was her time to be fully present with her family. It was non-negotiable for her, and though I didn't fully understand it at the time, I respected it. Now, I live by similar values. I align my day with what's important to me and plan accordingly.

Of course, life still throws unexpected challenges, and there are moments when we must respond to unplanned situations. But the difference now is that I'm not living in a constant state of responsiveness, which has significantly reduced my stress.

Now that you've begun to recognize and quiet the loud voice of your inner critic, it's time to create space for that softer, truer voice to emerge. This voice, the one that's aligned with your deepest desires and intuition, often starts off as a whisper, especially if you've been used to living in a reactive state. It may feel unfamiliar or even untrustworthy at first, but it grows stronger the more you nurture it. Just like building a muscle, the more you practice tuning in, the more natural it will become.

You don't need to rush into it. Start small, listening to the subtle nudges and paying attention to how you feel when you follow them. As you begin to notice positive outcomes, you'll develop more trust in your inner guidance. This is all part of the self-care journey we've been exploring, a process that brings together the mental, physical, and spiritual aspects of your well-being.

To help you along this path, I've put together some soulful self-love rituals that have worked for me. You can pick and choose the ones that resonate with you, or add your own. The key is to make space for yourself every day to connect with your inner voice and nurture your soul.

# Soulful Self-love Rituals

Here are some of the rituals and practices that have worked for me. Feel free to pick and choose or add what works for you.

- **Daily reflection time:** Make a little time each day to tune into yourself. Reflect on your intentions, how you're feeling, and what you're aspiring to. Even a few minutes can help you reconnect with your inner world.

- **Mindful meditation:** Start small – just five minutes to sit still and quiet your thoughts. As you become more comfortable, gradually increase the time. Meditation can help centre and calm your mind.

- **Gratitude journaling:** Write down three things you're grateful for every day. It's a simple practice, but it shifts your focus from what's not working to what is, reminding you of the blessings already present in your life.

- **Personal affirmations:** Create affirmations that speak to your heart. These personal mantras are a great tool to use when you're feeling challenged or need a little boost to get back to your true self.

- **Regular digital detox:** Choose a time – maybe one evening per week – to disconnect from your phone, emails, and social media. Unplugging allows you to reconnect with your thoughts and recharge your spirit.

- **Engage in creative expression:** Whether it's drawing, writing, singing, or dancing, give yourself permission to be creative. Let your soul express itself through whatever form feels most natural to you.

- **Nature immersion:** Make it a point to get outside regularly, even if it's just for a short walk. Nature has a way of grounding you and helping you reconnect with your inner peace.

- **Attend workshops/retreats:** Consider going to a retreat or workshop that aligns with your personal growth journey. These can be wonderful opportunities to deepen your connection to yourself and learn new tools.

- **Seek mentorship or guidance:** If it feels right, find a mentor or guide who can help you along your path. Having someone who understands your journey can offer insight and encouragement.

- **Practice active listening:** When you're in a conversation, give your full attention. Active listening nurtures deep, meaningful connections with others and helps you stay present.

- **Read inspirational literature:** Pick up a book or article that uplifts your spirit. It's a great way to nourish your mind and soul with new ideas and perspectives.

- **Cultivate a supportive community:** Surround yourself with people who understand and support your spiritual journey. A strong community can remind you that you're not alone in your pursuit of soulful living.

- **Prioritize self-care:** Tending to your soul is just as important as ticking off your to-do list. Schedule your self-care with the same priority as you would a business meeting – it's non-negotiable.

This checklist is about nurturing your inner world so that you can show up as the best version of yourself. It's a reminder that soulful living isn't something we do once in a while, it's a daily practice.

I encourage you to give this a shot. Dedicate as little as five minutes a day to a soul connection practice. This practice has allowed me to show up at work in a way that feels good for me. I'm more in control of my time, which allows me to be more productive. The connection to my inner voice has brought me more clarity and confidence in decision-making. I've tapped into it during challenging times to remind me to stay anchored to my desires, and I've been able to show up as a leader, colleague, mother, friend, and in so many other roles, as my most authentic self. This creates a ripple effect of positivity because when you shine your own light, you give others permission to do the same.

This is the beginning of your journey to truly becoming self-aware.

# Recap of Pillar 1: Love Yourself

Self-care is the essential first step towards loving yourself fully. It's about more than pampering or indulging in feel-good activities – it's about creating habits that support your entire well-being, allowing you to become more resilient and effective in both personal and professional aspects of life. This pillar reminds us that self-care is the foundation for thriving, helping us to stay grounded during challenges and energized during times of ease.

## *Reprogramme Your Mind: Shifting Thought Patterns for Success*

Your mind has a powerful influence on how you experience the world and how you show up in it. The thoughts you think repeatedly become patterns that shape your behaviour, often without you even realizing it. Reprogramming your mind is about breaking free from those negative, self-sabotaging thought patterns and creating new, more supportive beliefs.

## *Nourish Your Body: Honouring the Physical Vessel*

Self-care extends beyond the mind – it's also about taking care of your physical body, which is the foundation for all your experiences. Nourishing your body means treating it with the respect and care it deserves, so you have the energy and strength to live life fully and pursue your goals.

## Connect with Your Inner Self: Tuning into Your Inner Guidance

The third aspect of self-care focuses on connecting with your Inner Self. It's your intuition, your inner voice, and that part of you that knows your true desires. This connection is often neglected in the professional world, but it's essential for aligning your actions with your deepest values and finding true fulfilment.

## Love Yourself – Mind, Body, and Soul

The journey of self-care is about integrating the needs of your mind, body, and soul. When you take care of your mind by reprogramming negative thoughts, nourish your body with what it needs, and connect with your inner self, you create a powerful foundation for a life that feels balanced and fulfilling.

Each element supports the others – mental resilience allows you to handle challenges that come up in your physical practice, and a strong connection to your inner self helps you stay motivated to nourish your body and mind. This holistic approach to self-care empowers you to show up more authentically and effectively in every aspect of your life. It enables you to make decisions that align with your true self, maintain energy and focus, and create deeper, more meaningful connections with others.

Self-care isn't a one-time achievement; it's an ongoing commitment to loving yourself fully. Start with small, consistent practices and trust that every step brings you closer to a life that feels aligned, joyful, and true to you.

# Pillar 2

# Know Yourself

---

*The world will ask you who you are, and if you do not know, the world will tell you.*

– Carl Jung

For the first time in a long time, I wasn't just surviving; I was living. I felt grounded. I felt ease, and calm, and wellness was now a priority in my life. This went on for months as I deepened my practices and began to notice the benefits of this new lifestyle.

Although I now had the tools to manage stress and be more compassionate with myself, the situations that triggered the stress in the first place continued to exist.

Why did I feel like I was always putting out the same fires?

Sure, I had the tools and the routines to handle the chaos and rise above it. But why wasn't I truly happy?

I was in the stable life mode now. I had slowed down to take care of myself and the ease and gentleness were exactly what I needed at that time. But now I knew it was time to speed things up again towards a life that felt more driven and purposeful. I was searching for a happier version of myself. I wanted to live the life of that future self I imagined on Island B. I wanted to experience the fullest expression of myself and although I had already started the work with tapping into my core desired feelings, there was still more work to be done.

That's when I embarked on a journey of self-discovery to find out who I really am. The concept that I didn't already know myself seemed ludicrous to me initially. I had heard people say 'be your authentic self', but I didn't understand what that meant. How am I not being me? Who else can I be other than me? Whoever I was, I knew I needed a change.

I finally got it as I started to unravel the pieces of me through the self-discovery journey that I describe in this pillar. I wasn't being the real me. I was being the version of me that I thought I had to be to satisfy others' needs. The version that was not in alignment with what was in my heart. I knew this was not a complete version of myself because I felt stuck, confused, and frustrated. The real me would feel content, complete, and joyful – that much I knew.

Self-discovery, for me, was like walking into an old room I had forgotten about. A room where there were mirrors, showing all the different versions of 'me' I'd become over time – shaped by what others expected, family duties, and my own ideas of success. I felt the weight of these roles that I didn't even remember choosing, roles that didn't match who I wanted to be.

I dug deep. The biggest discovery for me during this process was that it wasn't just about looking back or looking at a new version of myself. It was digging up and rediscovering something I had buried a long time ago.

Self-discovery is not just about who you want to become but who you've always been. This was a revelation to me. I didn't need to look for anything outside myself. I needed to amplify what was already there. The challenge is to peel back the masks that you've layered on top of your core – your true self. What is at the core of you that needs to be magnified?

I started questioning the stories I'd told myself about who I was and realized that many of them weren't my stories at all – they came from outside pressures.

As I looked closer, my true self started to show up. I saw what made me different, where I felt most alive, and what mattered most to me. Knowing this, a path became clearer. My path became less about fitting in and more about carving out my own space, using what I've got, and doing what feels right for me.

# What does it mean to know yourself?

When you know yourself, you have high self-awareness. You understand your personality, your strengths, and what matters to you. Knowing yourself is also understanding how you are being perceived by others.

## *Why does it matter?*

You've established some self-care habits, but there's still a sense of uncertainty, especially regarding who you are and what strengths you possess. You might feel uncertain about your path or how to use your personality and strengths to create a stable life. Through self-awareness, discovering your strengths, and aligning them with what matters, you gain a deeper sense of security in who you are and the choices you make.

Having self-awareness allows you to understand and put into words the way you feel inside and behave. When you have this understanding you are better able to make choices that are right for you. When you know what environment is best suited for your personality, you have autonomy and can choose what you want for yourself instead of being told by someone else. When you know your strengths you have the ability to spend more time using and mastering them and thereby unleashing your full potential. When you know what matters to you and what you value, you have purpose and drive. Having this awareness gives you the opportunity to create the life that you desire.

# Benefits of Having High Self-awareness

- The ability to set boundaries because you know what you want and don't want.

- The ability to take action on what you want because you have clarity. Clarity is the heart of action. A confused mind always says 'no'.

- Become better at decision-making because you have focus and direction.

- More self-confidence so you can trust your intuition, show up, and shine.

- It allows you to understand things from multiple perspectives, which improves relationships. You can better appreciate other people's personalities, strengths, and values instead of judging them.

- It gives you a feeling of being more purposeful. We all want to live purposefully and feel like we are doing something because we want to do not because we have to.

- You feel like you belong – you stop wandering because you've found that place where you fit in and it feels like home.

- Imposter syndrome doesn't exist because you find your strength that naturally separates you from the crowd.

So how do you become more self-aware?

**We're going to explore self-awareness through three key areas:**

1. your personality,

2. your strengths, and

3. your values and what matters most to you.

**What you need to know before you go on this journey:**

1. **An open mind is required:** If you approach this with scepticism, like I initially did – thinking that some of these self-discovery tools can't possibly reveal who you are – then you'll miss out on valuable insights. Keep an open mind, especially when it comes to feedback that might feel like criticism.

2. **This journey will stir up a lot of feelings:** You may experience emotions like denial, anger, or even regret. There will also be moments of clarity, surprise, and self-realization when you discover things about yourself that you knew deep down all along. This part of the journey will demand self-care, self-compassion, and self-acceptance.

3. **You have to be honest:** This process only works if you're committed to being truthful with yourself. Chances are, you've been operating from a false self-identity for some time, so it's important to discern what's genuinely true vs what you've been conditioned to believe.

4. **Bring your detective skills:** You're looking for clues that will lead you back to your authentic self. A curious mindset, asking the right questions, and diving deeper into your experiences will be crucial in uncovering those insights.

5. **Patience is key:** Self-discovery is not a sprint; it's a marathon. Allow yourself the time to reflect and grow. The layers of conditioning won't peel away overnight, so give yourself permission to go at your own pace.

6. **Embrace discomfort:** Growth often comes from stepping outside your comfort zone. As you explore deeper truths about yourself, you may encounter discomfort, but this is where real transformation happens.

7. **Consistency matters:** Regular reflection, journaling, and mindfulness practices will help you make meaningful progress over time. Small, consistent actions will lead to bigger breakthroughs.

8. **Be prepared for change:** As you gain more self-awareness, it's natural for your perspective, relationships, or even goals to shift. Welcome these changes as a part of your evolution.

9. **Celebrate your progress:** As you journey through this process, don't forget to acknowledge and celebrate your wins, no matter how small. It's important to stay motivated by recognizing how far you've come.

10. **Be kind to yourself:** This is a process of growth, not perfection. As you uncover truths about yourself, prastice self-compassion and avoid harsh self-judgement. You're evolving, and that's something to be proud of.

# 9
# Discover Your Personality: Embracing Your True Nature

*Maybe the journey isn't about becoming anything. Maybe it's about unbecoming everything that isn't really you, so that you can be who you were meant to be in the first place.*

– Paulo Coelho

I began my self-awareness journey with personality assessments. While I had taken a few in the past, especially during job interviews, I didn't give them much thought at the time. Truth be told, I viewed them as tests you could pass or fail when applying for a job. This time, however, I approached them with curiosity and fewer preconceived notions, ready to explore what they might reveal about me.

What I discovered was that my personality – the unique combination of thinking, feeling, and acting – directly influenced my personal reality, shaping the environment and situations I was experiencing. This was a eureka moment for me. I began to see how my personality traits, like being a people pleaser and a perfectionist, had me in a loop of thinking, feeling, and acting. That loop shaped my environment as I attracted situations and people that matched my low self-worth, further cementing my belief.

My journey of discovering how my personality shaped my reality wasn't immediate. For years, I operated on autopilot, driven by an image of success I had unknowingly created based on others' expectations and my own personality traits.

This understanding took me back to a moment in university, sitting with classmates in a coffee shop, planning out our perfect lives. We discussed how far behind we felt – planning the ideal number of children, weddings, and career achievements, imagining we'd already need to be madly in love to meet those timelines. I felt like I needed to catch up. I envisioned myself in a boardroom, in a high-powered position, presenting confidently and living a fast-paced, modern existence. That picture became my standard for success.

After a few years in the corporate world, reality hit. I realized I didn't want that fast-paced life after all. Instead, I was drawn to creativity, ease, and a slower-paced life where I could wake up to birds chirping instead of alarm clocks. But trying to stick to that perfect plan left me burned out. My relationships suffered when things weren't perfect. Life began happening unexpectedly, and I found myself going off-script. I moved in with my boyfriend, got pregnant after five years together, then got engaged, then cancelled the wedding, and even had another pregnancy in between. This was not what I had planned or the order in which I was supposed to do things.

Diving into self-awareness allowed me to let go of my rigid plans. I started to see that life was happening in front of me, and I was missing it by trying to make everything perfect so I could enjoy it. I had planted this idea of the perfect life, and it was making me feel inadequate. But the more I let go, the more I realized it was okay to live outside those ideals. I even saw people who had followed their perfect plans but were deeply unhappy.

The idea that your personality creates your personal reality is one that I fully understood now. Someone who always aims to please will inevitably feel resentful and be taken advantage of because they inadvertently create the conditions that make it easy for others to do so.

Once I realized this was part of my personality – an identity I had adopted as a pleaser and perfectionist – I was able to step back, recognize it, and stop it from ruling my decisions. Remember the mindset work we did in previous chapters? This is where you begin to unravel that false identity shaping your personality.

When we truly understand our personalities, we gain the tools to shape our environments. Understanding my personality allowed me to realize what conditions were right for me, and in turn, how to create those conditions. This gave me a sense of autonomy – the ability to take control of my life rather than passively allowing things to happen to me. When you know who you are and what you need, you stop being a victim of circumstance and start shaping your own reality.

Personality assessments gave me the vocabulary to describe myself, and this was just the beginning. As I began to understand my motivations, I read *Drive* by Daniel Pink, and it further deepened my understanding. Pink's research shows that people are most motivated when they have autonomy, mastery, and purpose. This resonated deeply with me. Through personality assessments, I had started to claim my autonomy, creating the right environment for myself. Mastery and purpose, of which Pink speaks, are key aspects of self-awareness that I'll dive into in this pillar.

By understanding our personalities, we take the first steps towards creating a life where we are not just surviving, but thriving.

# So, How Do We Start This Process?

It requires a double-sided approach: internal self-reflection and external feedback. This balance is crucial because, as I learned from reading *Insight* by Dr Tasha Eurich, only 10% of people who think they are self-aware actually are. The reason for this gap is that self-awareness isn't just about how well you know yourself – it's also about how others perceive you.

Internal self-awareness gives us insight into our own patterns, while external self-awareness offers a mirror, showing us how others experience us. True growth happens when we integrate both perspectives, learning to see ourselves clearly and adjust our behaviours accordingly.

This external feedback part of the process, as you can imagine, was difficult. We often shy away from asking for feedback about ourselves because we fear judgement or criticism. But it's a necessary part of the journey. Internal self-awareness – the understanding of your own thoughts, emotions, and behaviours – must be aligned with how others see you for true self-awareness to take shape.

Self-awareness is not just about understanding ourselves in isolation; it's about knowing how we interact with the world around us. Our personality influences our motivations, reactions, and the environments we create. When we lack this external perspective, we risk creating situations that don't suit our needs, which often leads to conflict, stress, and frustration.

I never considered myself an introvert. After all, much of my career had been in front of the camera. As a communications professional, I regularly delivered speeches and represented my company publicly. Being in these highly visible roles, I assumed introversion didn't apply to me. But, despite my outward-facing work, people still labelled me as an introvert, and for a long time, I didn't quite understand why.

The truth is, my preference for working alone and recharging in solitude was often mistaken for shyness or being unsociable. It wasn't that I didn't enjoy interacting with people – I did, but those interactions drained my energy. After work events or big meetings, I would feel depleted, and I needed time to retreat into my own space to recover.

This disconnect became even more apparent in my daily work life. I preferred to think deeply and work alone before sharing my thoughts with others. My job demanded constant collaboration, but interruptions from colleagues would disrupt my flow. Instead of communicating that I needed uninterrupted time to focus, I would avoid eye contact or put on a stern face, hoping they would leave me alone. My colleagues misinterpreted this as me being miserable or unsociable when, in reality, I just needed the space to recharge and get my work done.

It took some deep reflection to realize that my behaviour wasn't about being shy or withdrawn; it was about how I managed my energy. I simply needed quiet time to process my thoughts and work efficiently. Over time, I learned to communicate this need to others rather than letting them assume I was unhappy or uninterested. Understanding that I wasn't shy but rather someone who needed solitude to recharge was a breakthrough for me, both personally and professionally.

This is where external self-awareness becomes vital. When we align our inner understanding with how we're perceived by others, we create fewer uncomfortable situations and misunderstandings. We can show up in the world the way we intend, and others can perceive us in the same light. This alignment demonstrates true self-awareness.

# Here's What I Did to Uncover More about My Personality

## *Internal Self-reflection*

- Start by researching a few personality assessments – I've included the ones I took. There are so many now, and it's worth trying a few of them to see which language you like. Here's an important thing to note: these are not going to tell you exactly who you are. They will give you insights into patterns and words that may resonate with you. It's up to you to make sense of it. Some of what I read didn't quite apply to me, but tapping into that inner voice and being truthful with myself allowed me to pick out what I felt was an accurate reflection of me. Jot down the words that resonate with you. For example, I saw creative.

- Then I started looking for evidence of these personality traits in my life, both at home and work. I looked at where I showed up. I reflected on my behaviour and how I made decisions.

### How I see myself

- Describe how you typically behave in everyday situations (e.g. calm under pressure, creative, empathetic, analytical).

- What activities or situations energize me?

- What situations drain me?

- What situations or behaviours from others trigger strong emotional reactions in me?

- How do I typically respond to stress or frustration?

- What recurring patterns or habits do I notice in my personal or professional life?

## External Feedback

### How do others perceive me

- Ask at least three trusted individuals:

    - How would you describe my personality?

    - What stands out most with how I interact with others?

    - How do I typically handle stress or challenging situations?

    - When do you notice me at my best? What am I doing?

*Blind spots*

- What strengths or weaknesses do others see that I may not recognize?

- Are there areas where others' feedback consistently surprises me?

As you begin to gather these insights, you'll notice patterns emerging. You'll see whether they align with your current self-perception or challenge it. The key is to remain open and honest with yourself as you navigate these realizations. Once you've gathered this information, you're ready to move on to the next phase: creating the right environment to thrive.

# Creating the Right Environment for You

Once I understood my personality, I started claiming my autonomy by making conscious decisions about the environments in which I thrived, whether in my career or personal life. I began to build a life that suited who I was, rather than trying to fit into spaces that made me feel inadequate. Take small steps to take control of your environment, even if larger changes, like career transitions or shifts in family dynamics, aren't immediately possible. The key is to make adjustments in small but meaningful ways, making your day-to-day life feel more supportive and aligned with who you are.

## *Steps to Create a Supportive Environment*

1. **Create Personal Boundaries within Existing Structures**

   Identify specific situations that trigger stress, discomfort, or frustration (e.g. constant interruptions, lack of quiet time, or feeling overcommitted). Set clear, gentle boundaries around those triggers. For example, if you're overwhelmed by constant interruptions at work, set dedicated focus hours and communicate to colleagues that you'll be unavailable during that time. In a family situation, establish quiet time for yourself, even if it's just 15 minutes a day, to recharge.

2. **Tailor Your Routine**

   Reflect on when and how you're most productive or energized based on your personality traits (e.g. morning person vs night owl, working alone vs collaboratively). Adapt your daily schedule within the limits of your job or family life. If you're more creative or focused in the morning, start your day with tasks that require deep thinking or problem-solving. If evenings are your time to recharge, reserve that time for activities that nourish your personality (e.g. reading, journaling, or hobbies).

3. **Reframe Your Space**

   Personalize your physical environment to reflect your personality, which can help reduce stress and make you feel more grounded. Make small adjustments like decluttering your workspace, adding calming elements (plants, art, or soft lighting), or creating a space that feels inspiring or peaceful. Even in shared spaces, a small corner or a few personal items can make a difference in how you feel.

4. **Communicate Needs without Guilt:**

If you're a people pleaser or feel pressured to say 'yes' to everything, practise communicating your needs in a positive, constructive way. Start small by saying 'no' to one non-essential task per week, or ask for help when needed. You can frame it by saying, 'I work best when I have some quiet time' or 'I'd love to help, but I need to finish [X task] first.'

5. **Find Micro-communities**

Seek out people in your current environment (colleagues, friends, or family members) who share similar values or personality traits. Foster those relationships to create a mini-support system. For example, at work, you might find colleagues who enjoy working quietly like you, and you can create a routine where you work together without interruptions. In a family, find common interests with a loved one to engage in activities that energize you.

6. **Prioritize Self-care Activities That Align with Your Personality**

Make space for activities that nourish your personality, even in small doses, to offset stress or challenges in your environment. If you're creative, carve out time each week for a hobby or project that lets you express that side of yourself. If you thrive on routine, create simple, predictable rituals (e.g. morning coffee, evening walk) to centre yourself amidst chaos.

7. **Celebrate Small Wins and Adjust Over Time**

Implement these changes gradually and reflect on what's working and what's not. At the end of each week, jot down what worked well and what could be adjusted to suit your personality better. This small reflection will help you make gradual, conscious shifts towards thriving in your environment.

# Recommended Resources to Help You

1. **Myers-Briggs**

www.16personalities.com

The Myers-Briggs Type Indicator (MBTI) identifies personality preferences based on four dimensions:

- Introversion (I) vs Extroversion (E)

- Sensing (S) vs Intuition (N)

- Thinking (T) vs Feeling (F)

- Judging (J) vs Perceiving (P)

This assessment provides insight into how you prefer to interact with the world and process information, offering guidance on communication styles, decision-making, and personal growth.

2. **StandOut Assessment**

https://www.loveandwork.org/standout

Developed by Marcus Buckingham, co-creator of StrengthsFinder, the StandOut Assessment distils nine roles that we naturally fit into based on our strengths and tendencies. I found this assessment extremely accurate. Like all these tools, it helps provide language to express how you feel and behave. It's especially useful for improving communication with others and setting boundaries that align with your personality.

3. **Enneagram**

www.truity.com

The Enneagram categorizes personalities into nine types, each defined by core motivations, fears, and world views. This assessment offers deep insights into how you respond to life situations, helping you better understand yourself and those around you.

4. **DISC Assessment**

www.123test.com

DISC analyses behaviour in four areas:

- Dominance

- Influence

- Steadiness

- Compliance

This tool is helpful in understanding your work style and how you interact with others, particularly in team environments.

5. **Entrepreneur Dynamics**

www.geniusu.com

Entrepreneur Dynamics helps you understand your business personality by identifying where you naturally add the most value within a business or entrepreneurial setting. This assessment is valuable not only for personal insights but also for guiding your role in a team or venture. It will be particularly useful in the next chapter on strengths, as it helps align your natural flow with your strengths to scale your success and impact.

While I utilized various assessments and tools to gain clarity, they only provided a framework. They granted me a vocabulary, a starting point. But I didn't let them dictate my entire narrative. Some insights resonated deeply, while others were points of reflection.

This is an important lesson as you dive deeper into self-discovery. These tools and assessments are just that – tools. They can offer insights, but they don't hold your complete story. We are all dynamic and ever-evolving. As we have new experiences and gain new knowledge, our understanding of ourselves deepens and shifts.

Remember that the journey of self-awareness is deeply personal and ongoing. While external inputs can guide and offer clarity, only you can carve out your unique path. Along the way, you'll find tools and signposts to assist you. However, at its core, it's about stitching together the puzzle pieces of who you are, informed by insights but driven by self-reflection and experience.

# What Insights Did You Gain from the Personality Assessments?

Write down what you learned about yourself. Use the self-reflection map I provide from www.theselflovemindset .com.

This template will serve you throughout this entire pillar of self-awareness. Keep it close by because in the next chapter we will be moving on to explore the role our strengths play in becoming more self-aware and being intentional with creating environments that help us strengthen those strengths towards self-mastery.

# 10

# Identify Your Strengths: Unlocking Your Unique Gifts

*Use the talents you possess, for the woods would be very silent if no birds sang except the best.*
— Henry Van Dyke

Whereas our personalities reflect how we naturally engage with the world, shaping how we behave, and which environments we thrive in, strengths are more about what we are good at or where we excel, often based on innate talent, experiences, developed skills, or learned abilities.

I was always someone who was very sceptical about psychometric or personality tests until I couldn't deny the results. These tests were sometimes able to articulate things that I couldn't put into words myself. They also gave me confirmation on things that I had suspected but chose to deny. For example, I liked to think of myself as someone who was detail-oriented, but the truth is, I am far from that. As a matter of fact, it's one of my greatest weaknesses. At first, I struggled to accept some of the findings, especially the realization that I'm not a detail-oriented person. That truth had never occurred to me before, but when I reflected on my frustrations – whether editing documents or managing minute details – it all started to make sense.

I tried really hard to get better at this because growing up, in both school and work, I was told there was always something about me that needed improving. There was always a weakness that needed strengthening. It's funny how our strengths, the things we are good at, get tossed to the sidelines because we are already operating optimally in those areas. Instead, our weaknesses are highlighted, making us feel like we're lacking, that we're not enough.

I had spent most of my life trying to improve the things I wasn't good at, which kept me stuck in a place of mediocrity. We're often made to feel like we need to be better simply because we don't excel at everything or aren't as 'well-rounded' as we're told we should be. Why not celebrate ourselves for who we are and strengthen our strengths? Why not strive for self-mastery instead of mediocrity?

We've been conditioned to ignore our strengths because we are doing just fine there, which means we don't spend time trying to master something. Instead, we spend our time trying to improve ourselves in areas we are destined to fail at or that will be a miserable and hard road towards success. A growth mindset suggests that we can become proficient at those other things, but when we spend so much time working on our weaknesses, it can become frustrating, and that's precisely why people burn out. It is stressful and hard.

That's why we get so frustrated trying to replicate the success of others by doing exactly what they did. The truth is that one person's winning strategy may be another person's losing strategy. Your personality, coupled with your strengths and values, will determine the winning strategy for you.

I was on a quest to uncover my winning strategy because the work I was doing wasn't entirely fulfilling, and Mondays did, in fact, feel like a drag. Like me at the time, many people are doing work they aren't engaged with and are creating businesses that are not the right fit for them. So, I dived in head first to discover my strengths.

Strengths, I discovered, are composed of three essential ingredients:

1. **Your talents:** Innate abilities you were born with.

2. **Skills:** Abilities you developed through practice and learning.

3. **Zone of genius:** The unique way you approach problem-solving, combining your talents and skills.

For me, one of the most transformative turning points was understanding the difference between talents, skills, and what I now recognize as my zone of genius. Gaining clarity on these nuances shifted how I saw myself and how I showed up in the world. Through this lens, I'm excited to share the insights that shaped my own growth, in hopes they might help you on your path as well. Let's jump straight into each.

# Talents

Talents are the abilities that come effortlessly to you. They are your natural gifts, the things you excel at without even trying. While others might struggle to achieve what comes easily to you, these abilities are what set you apart. In a way, they can be seen as your 'unfair advantage' – because while others may have to work hard to develop these skills, you already have a head start. This is not to say that talent alone is enough. To truly unlock the potential of a talent, you must put in the work to refine and perfect it. When you spend time cultivating and honing your natural abilities, those talents evolve into strengths. A strength is a talent that has been developed to a level of mastery.

The tricky part about identifying our talents is that, because they come so naturally, we often overlook them. It's easy to take for granted something that feels second nature, to the point where you might not even recognize it as a talent. For example, if you have a natural ability to communicate, organize, or think creatively, you might assume everyone can do these things just as easily. But in reality, these are talents that make you unique.

One of the best ways to discover your talents is to pay attention to what others consistently tell you you're good at. These are the areas where people often seek your help, advice, or guidance. Your talents are the things that, when others see you in action, they comment on how easy or natural it looks for you. This external feedback is a valuable clue in identifying your strengths.

To uncover your talents, think back on the compliments or feedback you've received throughout your life. What are the skills or abilities people regularly acknowledge in you? What do friends, colleagues, or family members seek you out for? Often, our greatest talents are hiding in plain sight, and we just need a bit of detective work to bring them to light.

1.  **Feedback:** Start with conversations. Friends, colleagues, and mentors can offer an external view, highlighting strengths you might take for granted. Their perspectives can provide invaluable insights into how your natural abilities are perceived and where they shine brightest.

2.  **Assessments:** Tools like Gallup's StrengthsFinder or VIA Character Strengths can provide a foundational understanding, helping identify the innate talents that drive you.

3. **Reflection:** Dedicate time for introspection by asking yourself probing questions. Analysing these moments can provide a clearer picture of where your talents reside.

- What have you been praised for?
- What do you find easy to do and people say you do effortlessly?
- What do you spend most of your time doing?
- What do people always ask you for help with?
- What do people tell you you're good at?
- What activities cause you to lose track of time?
- When do you feel most fulfilled?

# Skills

Skills are abilities you've acquired through experience and practice. Unlike talents, which come naturally, skills are developed over time through formal education, work, or personal interests. These are tangible abilities you can list on your resume – ranging from technical expertise to project management – but they also extend beyond the workplace. Hobbies, personal projects, and life experiences can help build valuable skills.

When reflecting on your skills, consider everything you've learned through different phases of your life – whether from school, jobs, courses, books, or hands-on practice. Skills are a product of effort and learning, and they can always be improved or expanded. For instance, if you've taken a cooking class or taught yourself coding, those are skills you've intentionally developed.

I recall a time in my corporate career when I had just started a new job as a Marketing Manager. I presented my strategy to the board and thought I nailed it. I was feeling good, confident that I'd communicated my ideas clearly and effectively. However, during a debrief with my manager afterward, he asked me where I thought I could improve. Feeling certain, I said, 'Well, I think my presentation skills are strong, so there's not much to improve there.' To my surprise, he disagreed.

At first, I was floored. I had always considered presenting one of my key skills. But after reflecting on his feedback, I realized that while I had a natural talent for speaking and delivering ideas, my presentations needed further refinement to become truly effective. This moment taught me that even skills we feel confident about can always be developed further. My ability to present wasn't fully realized because I hadn't yet put in the work to elevate it from a skill to a polished strength.

The lesson here is that skills are ever-evolving. Even if you think you've mastered a particular area, there is always room for growth. Just as my presentation skills needed further development, the same applies to any skill you've acquired. The key is to keep practising, keep learning, and never stop improving.

# Get Feedback

Ask the people you've worked with – friends, family, or colleagues – what skills they think you excel in and where they've noticed room for improvement.

# Make a List of All the Skills You've Acquired

Here are some prompts to help you:

- What are your qualifications?

- What books have you read?

- What courses have you taken?

- List your job history and think about the tasks you used to do.

# Categorize Your Skills

Not all skills are created equal – some energize us, while others drain us, even if we're good at them. Kristin A. Sherry's *YouMap* offers a framework for classifying skills into three categories or 'buckets'.

1. **Motivating skills:** These are the skills you're not only good at but also enjoy using. They energize you and make you feel fulfilled. For example, if you love problem-solving or brainstorming creative solutions, you'll feel energized every time you get to use that skill.

2.  **Burnout skills:** These are the skills you might be highly competent in, but they drain your energy. You can do them well, but doing them too often leaves you feeling depleted. For instance, you might be great at project management, but if it's not something that excites you, managing multiple projects daily might lead to burnout.

3.  **Developmental skills:** These are the skills you've identified as areas for growth. You might not be particularly good at them yet, or you might feel neutral about them, but there's room for improvement. For example, you might not be an expert in public speaking yet, but you see how developing that skill could propel you forward in your career or personal life.

Understanding these different types of skills was eye-opening for me. It allowed me to recognize where I should focus my energy and where I needed to set boundaries. Before this, I often found myself stuck doing work that I was good at but didn't particularly enjoy – work that fell into the burnout skills category. Recognizing this distinction gave me permission to prioritize the skills that truly motivated and energized me, while being mindful of how much time I spent on the draining ones.

By putting my skills into these buckets, I could see clearly where I needed to invest more time and effort and where I needed to pull back. This approach helped me feel more in control of my time and energy, ultimately leading to a more balanced way of working and living.

# Identify Your Burnout Skills, Motivating Skills, or Development Skills

1. **Detach yourself from the outcome and focus on the journey.**

   Start tracking the tasks that you do and notice how you feel while doing the work. Try not to think about the result or how people will feel about the outcome. Just focus on you and your energy while using those skills.

2. **Make a list of all the tasks/activities you do and track whether they give you energy or not.**

   It's okay to have tasks that you were great at and loved to do earlier in your life but no longer enjoy. We are evolving, dynamic people, and as we grow and gain new experiences, our preference for skills and tasks may change. Just because you loved it once doesn't mean you have to love it now. Be brutally honest with yourself. From the list of skills, circle the ones that you prefer, the ones that burn you out, and the ones that you'd like to develop.

# Zone of Genius: Discovering Your Magic

When I first encountered the idea of the 'Zone of Genius', it helped me understand how my skills and talents converged into something truly unique. Your genius is the way you think and solve problems in a manner that feels both effortless and energizing.

In his book *The Big Leap*, Gay Hendricks describes four zones that can help us categorize our activities and skills, ultimately giving us greater insight into how we work best. His four zones are:

1. **Zone of Incompetence**

   This is where you struggle with tasks that others can do far better than you. For me, this includes things like accounting or playing musical instruments. These aren't areas where I'm naturally inclined, and I tend to feel drained when I spend too much time here.

2. **Zone of Competence**

   These are tasks you can do well enough, but others are just as good at them. For me, this might be something like building websites – it's a skill I've picked up, but it's not where I truly shine. This is often where developing skills may land, but it's important to recognize that competence doesn't mean passion or energy.

3. **Zone of Excellence**

   These are the tasks you're highly skilled at and better at than most people. The tricky part here is that while you may be excellent at these things, they don't necessarily bring you joy. This is where

I found many of my burnout skills lived – things I was great at but didn't truly love doing.

4. **Zone of Genius**

This is where your true genius lies. These are the tasks that feel like second nature, where time flies because you're in your element. In this zone, you're not just good – you're exceptional. And not only that, you love doing it. For me, my genius lies in bringing clarity to confusion, rising above chaos, and unpacking big ideas into actionable steps. These are the activities that light me up and make me feel alive.

The challenge we often face is that we spend too much time in zones that drain us, particularly the zones of incompetence and competence. My goal became to spend as much time as possible in my Zone of Genius.

When I did this exercise myself, it became clear that I needed to delegate more, both at work and at home. I realized I was spending way too much time on tasks in my Zone of Incompetence, which was a poor use of my energy. I could have easily delegated those tasks to someone for whom that work was in their Zone of Genius. Take accounting, for example – anything numbers-related isn't my strong suit. I needed a strong finance person on my team to handle budgeting and the details. Even on a simpler note, things like blow-drying my hair – something I thought I could save time and money on by doing it myself – ended up wasting my energy. After spending hours trying to style my hair, I finally realized I should just go to the salon and have a professional handle it in half the time.

All of this is to say, once you start categorizing these tasks, it becomes clear how much time and energy we waste in zones that aren't optimal for us. It's not only a disservice to ourselves but to those around us as well. The more time we spend outside our Zone of Genius, the more stressed and frustrated we become, and that can lead to snapping at others or showing up in ways that don't reflect who we really are.

This exercise was a game-changer for me, both in my professional and personal life. It made me more conscious of how I was spending my time and where my energy was going.

To help deepen this process, I also turned to insights from Laura Garnett's work on the Zone of Genius. She emphasizes tracking your energy levels throughout the day to pinpoint when you're truly in your zone. I found this to be incredibly helpful in identifying those moments where I was fully engaged and intellectually stimulated.

### Here are some ways to discover your Zone of Genius

- **Energy tracking:** For a month or so, jot down tasks or projects that energize you. You'll start to recognize patterns, and this will give you a clear picture of where your genius lies.

- **Ask yourself these questions**
  - When are the moments that I'm in the zone and clearly intellectually stimulated and on fire?
  - What type of thinking or problem-solving am I doing to get those feelings?
  - When am I clearly out of the zone, bored, or frustrated and distracted?

- **Feedback:** Ask friends, colleagues, or mentors what they think you excel at effortlessly.

- **Deep dive into resources:** I highly recommend exploring books like *The Big Leap* by Gay Hendricks or insights from experts like Laura Garnett. These resources can provide frameworks and exercises to help you hone in on your unique genius.

Once you've gained insights into your strengths – your talents, skills, and Zone of Genius – the real work begins: integrating them into not only your life but also your business. For me, this started by assessing the tasks I could delete, delegate, or do in my personal workflow and as part of managing my team.

This audit, as simple as it is, was a real game-changer for me. The turning point came when I realized that to unlock both personal and professional fulfilment, I needed to prioritize working in my Zone of Genius and empower my team to do the same.

I remember going into the office for a strategy meeting and shifting the focus to my team, asking them about their talents, skills, and what they believed their Zone of Genius was. This exercise was an eye-opener for all of us. For instance, one team member, who was great with numbers, mentioned how much she loved solving problems in spreadsheets. I had spent hours struggling with a complicated budget for a proposal, feeling guilty for asking her to check my work. But here she was, saying she actually got excited about finding errors and fixing them – it was her Zone of Genius. If I had known that earlier, I could have saved myself time and frustration while giving her more opportunities to work in her zone.

I looked at what tasks drained my energy and started delegating or outsourcing those to people whose genius aligned with those areas. I started looking at team-building in an entirely different way. I didn't need someone who thought like me; I needed people who could add value where I had incompetencies. On a more practical level, I even outsourced things like blow-drying my hair, recognizing that it was worth freeing up my time for the things I was truly exceptional at.

The more time I spent operating in my Zone of Genius, the more productive and fulfilled I became. I empowered my team to do the same by identifying their talents and aligning them with the right roles. It not only improved their engagement but also elevated the entire business and team morale. When you and your team are working from your strengths, you're driving the business forward with energy, creativity, and focus.

The same concept applies if you're an entrepreneur. When you first started your business, chances are it was because of a specific talent or skill you had. Maybe you're an artist, a baker, or a tech expert, and you saw an opportunity to turn your passion into something bigger. But as your business grew, you likely found yourself doing far more than just that thing you love – your Zone of Genius. Now, you might be spending only a third of your time on what lights you up, while the rest is filled with customer service, paying bills, managing employees, and handling social media marketing.

The key to scaling your business is to stop doing everything yourself and start playing to your strengths and those of your team. By focusing on what truly energizes you and finding ways to delegate or eliminate tasks that drain you, you create the space to grow both personally and professionally.

It's about using these insights and knowledge about yourself to guide your professional choices, personal projects, and even your day-to-day tasks. This isn't about fitting into a box and staying there, as over time, you will evolve, gain new skills, perhaps discover new talents, and your Zone of Genius may shift or become more defined. The point here is to stay open and curious, knowing that you are dynamic and ever-evolving. So, be gentle with yourself as you work towards the fullest, most beautiful expression of who you are.

In the next chapter, we'll explore how to connect with what truly drives you, giving your strengths deeper meaning. We'll look at how this connection can shape your purpose and guide the impact you want to make in the world.

# 11

# Define What Matters: Clarifying Your Core Values

*Don't ask yourself what the world needs. Ask yourself what makes you come alive, and go do that. Because what the world needs is people who have come alive.*

— Howard Thurman

Once you've identified your strengths, the next step is discovering something that will sustain your motivation and drive, especially during challenging times. It's not enough to simply know what you're good at – you need to connect that with something that truly matters to you. This connection is what will keep you going when things get tough.

I discovered this almost by accident while working with colleagues who had completed the same life and health coaching programme as I did. Many were moving into the startup phase of their businesses but were struggling with the business side of things. Given my background in business and helping entrepreneurs with marketing, I knew I could offer value.

The biggest hurdle they faced was finding and articulating their niche – what problem they were solving and how they stood out in the market. Many of the individuals I worked with were driven by something personal – a challenge they had faced or a struggle they had overcome. They wanted to help others who were a few steps behind them on a similar journey. That's when it hit me: finding what matters isn't just about work or business – it's deeply personal. It's about finding where you can make the most meaningful impact based on your own experiences.

This led me to a deeper realization about purpose. Purpose didn't have to feel as intimidating as I had once thought. For years, I felt like I didn't fit in, constantly wondering what my purpose was. I felt confused and even lost at times, desperately seeking clarity. People often told me to 'follow my passion', but I had so many passions, how could I possibly choose just one? My confusion was compounded as I would start and stop projects the moment a brilliant new idea popped into my head. For some, identifying a passion can feel impossible, leaving them feeling like they're failing at life. I certainly felt that way.

For many of us, finding your why or your purpose can feel overwhelming. For me, the idea of purpose felt too big, like it was an all-or-nothing decision. As a multi-passionate, entrepreneurial-minded person, it was difficult to choose just one thing. Was my purpose tied to one of my many business ideas, the job paying the bills, or my passion projects and volunteer work? How could I possibly commit to just one thing when I had so much to give? I spent years searching for that one thing I was meant to do, only to be filled with anxiety about getting it wrong.

As someone with multiple passions and interests, I didn't want to be boxed into just one thing. What I eventually realized was that your purpose doesn't have to be about one singular thing – it's about identifying the string that ties together your personality, strengths, and experiences. That string is about finding something that matters to you personally, no matter what role you're in.

Whether you're a leader, part of a team, or an entrepreneur, this applies to all of us. It's not just about doing tasks or completing projects; it's about solving problems that resonate with you. Just like in business, where we often talk about solving customers' pain points, in life, the problems we feel most driven to solve are often tied to our own emotional experiences. This connection fuels our drive and ensures that our work feels relevant and fulfilling.

Many people start out passionate about their roles or projects but, over time, they can lose that connection to what originally inspired them. It's not uncommon to feel disconnected from your work or your life for that matter. This is why it's so important to ground your work, whatever it may be, in something personal and meaningful, not just practical or profitable.

At our core, I believe we all want the same thing: to feel like we belong, to know that our lives matter, and to find our place in the world. We want to wake up every day with a sense of purpose, but often we get caught up in chasing external achievements, titles, accomplishments, or credentials that leave us feeling unfulfilled. True fulfilment, however, comes when we use our strengths to solve a problem that matters to us, in service of something bigger than ourselves.

# Discovering Your Personal Niche

This concept of finding your personal niche emerged through the work I was doing, recognizing that it applies to all of us, whether we're entrepreneurs, employees, or leaders.

So, what matters to you most? Is it helping others feel seen and heard? Is it supporting people to make better decisions? Is it giving others a platform to share their voice?

The strongest connection you'll find is often through your values and personal experiences that have shaped you. I've found, through my own journey and the journeys of others, that what matters most to us is often connected to our own struggles or challenges. These are the experiences that create a strong emotional connection and often drive the most meaningful work.

Just as businesses solve customer pain points, in life, we solve problems that resonate with our own struggles. It's in these personal pain points that we can often find what drives us. Whether it's something we've overcome ourselves or something that has affected someone close to us, it's these connections that fuel our motivation and give our work a deeper meaning.

This is why doing work that is meaningful to you is so important. It's what allows you to show up every day and stay committed, even when times are tough. Whether you're an employee dealing with a difficult project, a leader navigating challenges, or an entrepreneur building something from the ground up, connecting to what truly matters to you will give you the drive to keep moving forward.

## *Discovering What Matters*

1. **Start with Identifying Your Values**

   Values are the foundation for what truly matters to you, guiding how you apply your strengths. While strengths define what you're good at, values give them direction and meaning. When your actions – whether in the work you do or how you live your life – align with both your strengths and values, it creates a deeper sense of purpose and motivation, allowing you to stay driven even during challenging times. This alignment helps you focus on what's important, making your efforts more fulfilling and impactful.

   **Values Reflection and Prioritization**

   · **Reflect on meaningful experiences**

     Think of three to five significant moments in your life (personal or professional) when you felt fulfilled, proud, and purposeful. What values were at play in those moments? For example, was it connection, achievement, compassion, or integrity that made them meaningful?

- **Identify common themes**

  Look for patterns or recurring values across those moments. Which values keep showing up? These are likely your core values.

- **Select and rank core values**

  From the values you've identified, choose 5–10 that resonate most with you and rank them in order of importance. This will help you identify which values guide your decisions and bring the most fulfilment.

- **Apply values to decision-making**

  Reflect on how your values currently show up in your work or personal life. Are you honouring them? What adjustments could you make to align your actions more closely with your core values?

2. **Reflect on Personal and Professional Experiences**

   Your past experiences often hold the key to what matters most to you. By reflecting on significant moments, both personal and professional, you can uncover patterns that point to your purpose and the things that truly drive you.

## Personal Reflection

- ### Reflect on childhood

  Think of three significant moments from your childhood or formative years that shaped who you are today. These can be moments of triumph, struggle, or learning.

- ### Look at your wounds

  Ask yourself, 'What wounded me?' This question encourages you to explore emotional pain points or difficult experiences that left a lasting mark on you. For example, was there a moment when you felt deeply misunderstood, unsupported, or unfairly treated? These wounds often shape your values and give insight into what matters to you now.

- ### Consider what bothers you deeply

  Reflect on the things that still bother or frustrate you deeply. These are often clues to your sense of justice, fairness, or passion. For example, is there a societal issue, workplace dynamic, or personal situation that consistently bothers you? These feelings usually reveal something important about what you care about and what drives you to take action.

- ### Review your work history

  What tasks, roles, or projects energized you, and which ones drained you? What did you enjoy and find fulfilling, and what did you dislike? This reflection can help you identify patterns in your professional life that connect to your core values.

- **Identify patterns**

  Look for recurring themes or experiences across your personal and professional reflections. What strengths, values, or passions show up repeatedly? These patterns can reveal important insights about what matters most to you and where you might find the most purpose.

3. **Find What Matters to You**

Once you've reflected on your past experiences and identified your values, the next step is finding what truly matters to you. This will help you create alignment between your personal values and your professional or personal pursuits.

**Reflection Questions**

- Are there people you're naturally drawn to serve – perhaps because they remind you of a version of yourself from years ago? These could be individuals facing challenges you've already overcome.

- Is there a personal situation or wound you've healed from that you now feel called to help others through? This could shape your purpose in your career, personal life, or volunteer efforts.

- Is there a problem you want to solve because it has personal meaning to you? Whether it's something that has directly affected you or someone close to you, this connection will help fuel your passion and drive.

## 4. Apply Insights to Your Purpose

Now that you've explored your values and reflected on your personal and professional experiences, it's time to connect these insights to your life and work. By aligning your strengths, values, and purpose, you'll have a powerful foundation to sustain motivation and fulfilment.

### Reflection Questions

- Who are the people you feel most called to serve? Are they facing challenges similar to those you've experienced in the past?

- What situation or problem do you feel most passionate about solving? How can your personal experiences inform the way you approach this?

- How can you integrate your values into your daily work or projects to stay aligned with what truly matters?

Think about how your strengths, values, and personal experiences intersect. What common thread ties them together? How can you use this insight to guide your next steps, whether it's in your current role, a new venture, or a personal project?

Let me ask you this: What would happen if we found what matters to us – our personal niche – that place where you feel like you belong, feel comfortable, and feel like you are on fire and ready to take on the day, doing activities that you love, using your unique strengths to solve problems that matter to you in service to people who matter to you?

We'd have

· happier people,

· more motivated and productive people,

· better leaders, and

· more people taking 100% responsibility for their happiness and well-being.

When we love ourselves through self-care and know ourselves through self-awareness, we can create value for ourselves and others. That's what we are going to be exploring in the next pillar: how we can take all that self-love we've begun to develop and extend love out into the world by being of service.

# Recap of Pillar 2: Know Yourself

Self-awareness is the second crucial step in the journey to loving yourself fully. It goes beyond simply recognizing your strengths and weaknesses; it's about gaining a deep understanding of who you are, what drives you, and how you engage with the world around you. Self-awareness allows you to align your actions with your true self, empowering you to make decisions that reflect your values and enhance your personal and professional life. This pillar reminds us that self-awareness is the key to personal growth, providing clarity and direction, and helping us navigate life with authenticity and purpose.

## *Personality:*

- Understanding your personality, how you're wired, and what kind of environment is best suited for you to thrive in.

- You would have completed several personality assessments to uncover the best environment for your true self to flourish.

## *Strengths:*

- Uncovering your strengths and having the ability to use, strengthen, and master them. In this chapter, you worked on discovering:

- Your talents – the natural abilities you were born with.

- Your skills – the abilities you have learned through practice.

- Your Zone of Genius – your unique way of thinking and problem-solving using your talents and skills.

## *Something that matters:*

- What are your values? What matters to you, and how can you spend more of your time doing things that align with your values?

- What values matter most to you?

- How have your childhood and personal experiences shaped and informed what matters most to you?

Now that you've aligned your personality, strengths, and what matters most to you, the final step is putting it all into action. In the third and final pillar of the self-love mindset, we'll explore how to **create value** – both for yourself and the world around you. We'll dive into how you can take your strengths and turn them into tangible contributions that serve others, whether in your personal life, work, or community. This is where your self-awareness and purpose come together to create a lasting impact. Let's move forward into **creating value**.

# Pillar 3

# **Create Value**

*Do your little bit of good where you are; it's those little bits of good put together that overwhelm the world.*

– Desmond Tutu

I felt calmer, clearer, and less scattered. I finally started to feel in control of my life without being controlling of others or circumstances. Communicating your needs without feeling shame, guilt, or resentment feels freeing.

I discovered that the authentic version of me was applying my skills, fuelled by my strengths and Zone of Genius, to do work that aligns with my values and what matters to me.

I had a eureka moment, and as simple as it sounds, it's truly a lesson I hope to help others experience through my work and this book. All the work I was doing to strengthen my weaknesses, pretending to know things I didn't (and quite frankly wasn't really interested in), just to appear to be something other than what I am, was futile. It was a waste of time and energy, as I would always be a mediocre version of someone else. No matter how hard I tried, I would never outshine them by trying to be them. That would never bring me joy or fulfilment. I didn't need to outshine anyone. I just needed to shine my own light. I could find my own greatness by mastering myself.

The challenge many people face is that they don't believe what they have to offer is great. That's why starting with self-care helped me to really love myself, develop self-compassion, self-esteem, and self-worth. I needed to change the way I thought about myself. That's the power of loving myself – you begin to realize that what you have to offer is good enough, no matter what it is.

I could clearly see that all this time, I was trying to be someone else. In school, we were told to do better at our weakest subjects, be more like that other kid who gets straight As, behaves well, or speaks up in class. In the workplace, this sentiment continues, asking employees to work on their areas for improvement and weaknesses.

I'm not saying there isn't room for growth and improvement, but the bigger message here is that we've been told to strengthen our weaknesses instead of mastering our strengths. We end up chasing this goal of perfection that is unattainable because we lose sight of who we are and what matters to us.

I saw other people's skills, talents, and ways of being and wanted to emulate that. There's nothing wrong with inspiration, but when you try to be someone else, you'll always be a mediocre version of them. They are already taken. They have their own innate talents, lived a different life, learned different skills, and have experiences that shape their values. When I realized that I could never be anything other than who I am, I committed to being the best version of myself, with no excuses, no apologies.

This journey, although personal, extends far beyond ourselves. The insights gleaned from it are not just stories; they're tools and strategies to navigate our demanding personal and professional lives. The knowledge that our well-being significantly influences our professional success is empowering. By focusing on individual well-being, we can create environments where businesses don't just succeed – they thrive, innovate, and grow, driven by individuals who are whole, content, and motivated.

When we prioritize our well-being, we're not just making a choice for ourselves; we're setting a precedent for our teams, colleagues, and everyone we interact with. It's a powerful statement that says, 'I value myself, and I value you.' This is the essence of *The Self-love Mindset*. It's a call to integrate our whole selves, to find personal happiness and well-being, and to inspire others to do the same.

I had built the foundation of well-being with self-care and self-awareness. But something still kept me up at night – a subtle pull towards something deeper, a need to make a bigger impact. This wasn't just about feeling good within myself anymore; it was about creating value in the world around me, beyond my own personal growth.

That's when I realized I was transitioning from a journey of self-awareness and security into something greater – a journey to significance. It was time to take everything I had learned about loving myself, trusting my strengths, and honouring my values and apply it to creating real, lasting value for others.

This opportunity became real when I was appointed CEO of one of Richard Branson's non-profits. All of my self-protecting patterns came to the surface again – those familiar feelings of not being good enough or worthy of such a role. But now, I knew better. I didn't need to fit into anyone else's mould or try to be like my predecessors. I realized I could create value just by showing up as my authentic self. This was the shift from self-awareness to service. It was the moment I stepped fully into significance, using my strengths, my voice, and my passion to create something meaningful for others.

I initially believed I had to choose between two parts of myself: the entrepreneurial businesswoman and the wellness advocate. It felt like these worlds were at opposite ends of the spectrum. However, I soon realized that by combining these two passions, I could create unique value. I didn't have to choose. Instead, I could merge these passions to build something even more meaningful.

I decided to create value by showing up as the real, authentic me – bringing my strengths and values into every decision. I wanted to be the 'Wellness CEO' who put a spotlight on well-being in life and business. My contribution would be to show that we can thrive in both worlds with a self-love mindset. This is the heart of creating value. Using your unique experiences and strengths to make a meaningful impact on the world around you.

As you begin this journey, ask yourself: How can you create value right where you are, with what you already have?

# What does it mean to create value?

Creating value means being of service to others by using your strengths.

## Why does it matter?

You've reached a level of security and comfort, but you may still feel like something is missing. You're not fully leveraging your potential to create impact and meaning in the world. The focus here is not just on security, but on finding significance. In this pillar, the journey shifts towards creating value and making a meaningful contribution – moving from personal security to significance, where you connect your strengths and purpose with serving others.

When you begin to create value for your community (friends, family, clients), you live a life of significance.

You feel fulfilled because you love what you're doing, and it feels good because it feels purposeful. Many times people do work that either doesn't utilize their strengths, which makes them feel inadequate, or they are doing work that is against their values, so they don't feel purposeful.

To create value for others that is authentic and feels good, it can't be done out of desperation for money or attention. When you love yourself, your motivation comes from within, so those external outcomes don't matter.

When you know yourself, you have drive and purpose. Now you have all the right ingredients to be of service to others. Creating value can show up in many ways – it could be volunteering in your community, creating a business by offering a service, making a product, offering new ideas to improve processes at the company you work for, or inspiring and empowering others through your own story.

Try changing the way you think about work from being a means to an end, and you'll soon see that once you create value for others, there is always an exchange – value for value. When you create value for others, you create value for yourself.

# Benefits of Creating Value

- **Sense of purpose:** Contributing to others gives you a deeper sense of purpose, aligning your actions with something greater than yourself.

- **Personal growth:** Service challenges you to grow, develop new skills, and expand your understanding of others' needs.

- **Connection and relationships:** Serving others strengthens relationships and fosters meaningful connections with your community, clients, or network.

- **Fulfilment and satisfaction:** Helping others brings a deep sense of fulfilment and inner satisfaction, enhancing your own well-being.

- **Enhanced reputation and influence:** Providing value through service builds trust, credibility, and influence, often leading to new opportunities.

- **Legacy building:** Through service, you leave a lasting impact on others, contributing to a legacy of positive change.

- **Reciprocal benefit:** The value you give often comes back to you in unexpected ways – whether through personal fulfilment, new partnerships, or shared success.

# So How Do You Create Value?

**Creating value and being of service** – Now that you've done the inner work, you have clarity and focus to take action.

We're going to dive into service, within the framework of the self-love mindset, with three core areas:

1.  **Mastering your message:** Your message is the guiding principle behind the value you create. It's what you stand for and what you offer to the world, based on your strengths, experiences, and passions.

2.  **Sharing your message:** Having a message is only the beginning – sharing it is how you create value in the world. The more you share your message, the more you attract opportunities and build influence.

3.  **Creating assets:** Creating assets is about turning your message into something tangible that continues to provide value. This could be products, content, or intellectual property that reflects your strengths and expertise. By building assets like a book, course, or system, you create long-term impact and generate ongoing value for yourself and others.

# 12

# Crafting Your Message: The Power of Your Personal Story

*What you say can inspire the world or diminish it. Choose your words wisely.*

— Robin Sharma

Once you've gained clarity, focus, and direction through self-awareness, it's natural to feel ready to jump into action. You may find yourself wanting to

- ask for a promotion,
- apply for jobs that better align with your strengths,
- take courses that further develop your talents,
- start a business that solves a problem you care about, or
- volunteer for projects that align with your values and make you feel purposeful.

Before taking any of these steps, it's essential to craft a powerful personal message that will guide your actions. Your message serves as the foundation for the value you create and allows you to move forward with clarity and intention.

I believe we all have a message to share with the world. Whether or not we are speakers, writers, or professional communicators, we each have a personal message – something that deeply matters to us. Your message allows you to clearly articulate what you stand for, bringing you clarity and direction in your work and life.

As I reflected on my past, I realized that my message was shaped by those early experiences. The belief that I wasn't worthy of love and the challenges my family faced. These moments cast me as a victim, yet they also ignited a desire to help others. Still, I spent much of my life trying to fix my weaknesses. As I grew older, I believed there was always someone better, someone I had to emulate. The more I pushed to achieve external success, to be more, to do more, and to earn more validation, the emptier I felt inside. It wasn't until life brought me to my knees, forcing me to prioritize my own wellness, that everything began to shift.

The moment I learned to love myself as I am, everything started to click. I stopped chasing approval and began attracting the right people and opportunities into my life. My message became clear: I have a story to share, and it's this one. It's this book. No matter what you've experienced or are currently going through, you are worthy of love and being loved. Love yourself, know yourself, and create value in the world by being authentically you. That's my message.

Your message helps you stay aligned with what matters to you most, making it easier to attract opportunities and connect with your community. But before you can effectively share it, you must first get clear about what that message is.

In life and business, you will be known for something, whether it's good or bad. The truth is, you can't serve everyone, and if you've done enough self-discovery, you realize you aren't meant to. You have a particular way of being and things that matter to you, and that's what will resonate with the right people – your community.

When you start being intentional with the message you put out into the world, you begin to be known for something, and you stand out for the right reasons. The reasons you want. This is you steering your ship in the direction you want.

I'm often asked to do interviews or give talks, and this started back when I worked in marketing. No matter how many times I did it, I always felt the nerves. I'd find myself studying notes like I was cramming for an exam, trying to remember everything I wanted to say. But the moment I gained clarity around my message, something shifted. It became easier to step on stage, sit down for an interview, or have a meaningful conversation. When you're sharing an idea you truly believe in, it flows naturally.

This clarity isn't just for public speaking – it applies to so many areas of life. Whether you're interviewing for a job, attending a networking event, sharing your vision, or building a business, communication is at the heart of it all. The key is this: You're not selling yourself, you're sharing your message. When you connect with what matters most to you, that authenticity shines through, and the words come with ease.

Your message becomes your focal point, allowing you to control the narrative. When you lead with your message, you become known for the things you care about, not just your title, credentials, or accomplishments.

If you're creative like me, you've dipped your toes into many projects, ideas, or ventures. I had a million and one things going on, and this left me feeling disjointed and scattered, especially when speaking to others about myself. My default response was always to mention my job or title. This, too, would leave me feeling less confident in the conversation. My job isn't who I am; it's what I do. I wasn't able to fully express what I stand for. The moment I got clear on my message, I avoided chaos, confusion, and shiny-object syndrome. My message of a self-love mindset gave me focus, clarity, and direction. The truth is that people are drawn to ideas and beliefs more than self-promotion, and that makes you a much more interesting person to talk to.

# The Impact of a Strong Message

- **Clarity of purpose:** A strong personal message provides clarity about who you are and what you stand for. It serves as a foundation for making decisions, whether in your career or personal life, ensuring that you stay aligned with your values and purpose.

- **Confidence in communication:** Knowing your message gives you confidence in expressing yourself. Whether in meetings, presentations, or casual conversations, you'll speak with conviction, making it easier to communicate your ideas persuasively and authentically.

- **Build meaningful connections:** A personal message helps you connect with others on a deeper level. By sharing what truly matters to you, you attract people who resonate with your values and vision, fostering genuine relationships both professionally and personally.

- **Resilience in challenges:** In times of difficulty or uncertainty, a strong message acts as a reminder of your 'why'. It grounds you, helping you navigate challenges with purpose and resilience, rather than feeling lost or overwhelmed.

- **Career advancement:** Having a clear personal message positions you as someone with a unique perspective. This can open doors for promotions, leadership roles, and new career opportunities as others recognize the value and insight you bring.

- **Consistency in actions:** A well-defined message helps you stay consistent in your behaviour, actions, and decisions. It creates alignment between what you say and what you do, building trust and credibility with others.

- **Personal fulfilment:** Living in alignment with your message brings a sense of fulfilment. When your actions reflect your inner values and beliefs, you feel more satisfied and purposeful in your work and life.

- **Influence and impact:** When you consistently live by your message, you naturally influence those around you. Whether you're in a leadership role or part of a team, your message can inspire others to follow suit, amplifying your impact on your community, workplace, or industry.

- **Emotional well-being:** Being clear about your message can reduce stress and anxiety. You no longer have to second-guess your choices or chase external validation because you're rooted in what matters to you. This sense of self-assurance contributes to a more peaceful, emotionally balanced life.

- **Empowerment to take action:** A strong personal message empowers you to take bold steps towards your goals. You're less likely to hesitate or hold back because you have a clear sense of what you're striving for and why it matters.

# Your Point of View: The Missing Piece

One of the most important aspects of your message is your point of view. Your perspective is what differentiates you and adds depth to your message. Now, not everyone is going to share your point of view, and you may get a lot of criticism for it, but it will resonate deeply with those who need to hear it. Your community wants to know your unique perspective because that's what makes your message valuable.

Taking a stand with your point of view allows people to understand what you stand for. This is why self-awareness is so crucial; it helps you know what truly matters to you so that you can confidently stand by your perspective, even if it isn't universally accepted.

Early on in my role as the CEO of the Branson Centre Caribbean, I shared my vision with someone, expressing that I wanted to be known as the 'Wellness CEO'. I wanted to be someone who made well-being a strategic business imperative. Their response was, 'You may want to think about that', implying that it wasn't a good idea. But I had my message, and I was clear about what I wanted to do. I wasn't deterred.

When you integrate your message with your unique point of view, you become a voice that others can rely on. You may not resonate with everyone, and that's okay. What matters is that you offer value to the people who need to hear your message.

This book is an extension of my message. Everything I've shared here reflects my belief that you can find happiness and fulfilment in life and business when you love yourself, know yourself, and create value. That's my message, and I've spent my journey aligning everything I do around it.

Whenever I do a talk, keynote, or speak with entrepreneurs and partners, I always carry my message with me. I remember one particular talk I was asked to give to a group of entrepreneurs competing in the electric mobility space. In a room full of energy and innovation executives, I found a way to weave in my message of self-care. At first, I wondered if it was too unexpected, but the response was overwhelmingly positive. People found it inspiring and refreshing to see that innovation starts with taking care of ourselves. Sure, there were a handful of people who weren't impressed, but that didn't faze me. What mattered was that I stayed true to my message. It was relevant, it was different, and it made me stand out.

People will often try to steer your message, especially when you're speaking on their stage, in their boardroom, or elsewhere. They'll suggest what you should say or how you should frame your ideas. This is why it's so important to be crystal clear about your message – so you can lead the narrative and not let others shape it for you. Standing in your truth is what makes your voice powerful.

Now that you understand the power of a message, it's time to start crafting your own. You've already done a lot of the groundwork in the previous chapter on self-awareness. You've explored what deeply bothers you, uncovered some of your childhood wounds or struggles, and identified problems you feel compelled to solve. Now, let's pull it all together and shape how your message can be shared with the world.

This exercise will help you take what matters to you and combine it with your strengths to craft a personal message. The idea is to use your experiences – what you've struggled with and what drives you – and connect that to how your strengths can contribute to solving those problems. Remember, your message will evolve and change over time, just as mine did. I started out speaking about finding your business niche, and that eventually evolved into the self-love mindset.

# Activity: Craft Your Message

To begin, reflect on the following questions. Answer them in this order to help clarify your message, knowing that it will grow as you do.

1. **What's the one thing you wish you had known when you were struggling?**

   Think about a time when you were in the midst of your biggest challenges – what advice or wisdom would have made a difference for you?

2. **What do you want people to remember you for?**

   Imagine looking back on your life or career. What legacy do you want to leave behind?

3. **What problem are you passionate about solving?**

   Consider the issues that light you up or make you angry. What's the cause or challenge you feel called to address?

4. **What values guide your actions?**

   Reflect on the core values that drive your decisions and behaviour. What are the principles that matter most to you?

5. **What is your unique perspective on this topic?**

   Everyone has a different lens through which they see the world. What makes your point of view on this issue distinct or valuable?

6. **How can you use your strengths to contribute to this message?**

   Identify the strengths you've uncovered in previous exercises. How can they help you make an impact in the area that matters to you?

Here's an example of what this exercise looked like for me:

- **What's the one thing you wish you had known when you were struggling?**

I wish I had known that taking care of myself wasn't a luxury but a necessity, and that self-love starts with prioritizing my own well-being.

- **What do you want people to remember you for?**

I want to be remembered for helping others realize that they can love themselves fully and that prioritizing self-care and self-awareness leads to a more fulfilling and impactful life.

- **What problem are you passionate about solving?**

I'm passionate about helping people, especially entrepreneurs and parents, break free from burnout and realize that they don't have to sacrifice their own well-being for success.

- **What values guide your actions?**

Freedom, authenticity, love, joy, compassion, courage, and balance.

- **What is your unique perspective on this topic?**

Having experienced burnout as both a mum and an entrepreneur, I learned that neglecting my own needs made everything harder. My journey to self-love taught me that taking care of myself first allowed me to show up better for others and create more value in my work and life.

- **How can you use your strengths to contribute to this message?**

  By using my strengths in communication and simplifying big ideas, I can teach others how to apply self-care and self-awareness in practical ways that feel achievable, helping them break down these concepts into actions that fit their lives.

Through my journey of overcoming burnout and learning to love myself, I've discovered that true success starts with self-love. My message is simple: love yourself through self-care, know yourself through self-awareness, and create value through service. This mindset has transformed my life, and I'm here to help others embrace the same path.

As you reflect on your experiences and strengths, remember that crafting your message isn't about perfection. It's about embracing your journey and sharing the value that only you can offer the world. With a clear message, you'll not only feel more empowered, but you'll also inspire others along the way.

That's what we're going to explore in the next chapter – how you can start sharing your message.

# 13

# Sharing Your Message: Amplifying Your Voice and Impact

*Your message could be the key that unlocks someone else's prison.*

– Joel Osteen

Once you've created your message, the next step is to share it with your community and the people who need to hear it. This is where you'll be spending a lot of your time, as sharing your message will become a natural part of your daily life. The more you speak about your message, the more confidence you'll build as you become more familiar with your topic and ideas. It will become very easy for you to speak about.

Sharing your message allows you to attract the right opportunities and make a meaningful impact. You don't need to be everywhere. In fact, you shouldn't be. You just need to be in the spaces that are right for you and your community. When you begin to share your message with intention, you naturally become a person of influence.

I never would have described myself as a person of influence at first, as I always thought that role was for someone who enjoys being in the public eye. I'm more reserved, and I've never felt comfortable sharing my personal life with the world, especially on social media. That doesn't come naturally to me. But what I did find easy was sharing the heart of my message, rather than details about my personal life. In doing so, I realized that being a person of influence isn't about public exposure; it's about the impact you have on those around you, especially in your own community.

Many of the personal stories I've shared in this book, I've kept to myself for a long time. I didn't see the need to talk about my insecurities, traumas, or setbacks. I'm a private person by nature. But I've come to realize the power in vulnerability, in releasing the shame I used to carry about my struggles. Through sharing these moments with intention, I've been able to connect more deeply with my community and offer the kind of support that truly resonates with them.

The work I've done on this journey has shown me that my story, with all its ups and downs, is a big part of who I am today. While there are still stories I hold close to my heart, I've learned that it's okay to be vulnerable. You never know who your story might help.

I remember sharing a story during one of my talks about a time I was crying under my desk, feeling completely helpless in my role. Afterward, an audience member came up to thank me for my honesty. She said not many leaders admit to having those vulnerable moments, and hearing my story made her feel like there was nothing wrong with being human. Moments like these remind me that influence isn't about fame or exposure – it's about making a genuine connection with those who need to hear your message.

Sharing your message allows you to connect with the people who can help you fulfil your mission, whether that's building a team, forming meaningful relationships, or simply finding someone who can open doors for you. This is a crucial aspect of both personal and professional growth.

Often, people tend to work in isolation, creating ideas or plans without sharing them, only to later realize they've been focused on the wrong audience or even missed the mark on what they truly needed. The best solution is to start sharing your message early – whether it's an idea, a goal, or a vision – and seek feedback on your thoughts and perspective. By doing this, you begin to engage and enrol your community.

This process helps you refine your message and connect with the two types of people essential to your journey:

1. **Supporters:** Those who will help you move your mission forward whether through guidance, collaboration, or opportunity.

2. **Beneficiaries:** The people who will directly benefit from your message, such as your audience, clients, or those who need to hear what you have to offer.

Whether from a business or personal perspective, sharing your message not only helps clarify your purpose, it also attracts the right people who will support and benefit from your vision.

When I started sharing my message, I knew I was onto something based on the feedback I was getting. People wanted to hear more and learn more. This was intriguing for me. I thought it was incredible that people actually wanted to listen to my point of view on a matter that was important to me. Even more incredible was that I was actually making a positive impact on people's lives just by talking! I didn't need to be or do anything other than be myself. This felt really great.

The more I shared my message, the more refined it became. It doesn't have to be perfect at first. What's important is that you begin. Just like any startup business, you have to start with an idea, test your minimum viable product in the market, and iterate as you get feedback.

The beauty of this process is that, even though you may have a message to share, there are people who will help you refine and shape it along the way. These could be teachers, mentors, family members, friends, colleagues, or even strangers. I've learned from all of them. Whether they introduced me to a new idea, recommended a book, shared valuable feedback, or simply connected me with the right person, they all played a role in helping me grow and apply what I learned to my journey.

Once you've begun refining your message, it's time to think about how you can expand your reach. One of the most effective ways to do this is by leveraging other people's platforms, as they've already built the communities you want to connect with.

# Leverage Other People's Audiences

I've learned that there are people whose mission is to open doors and put a spotlight on other people's messages. Look at Oprah – she has been a catalyst for so many others by simply providing a platform for them to share their message. After trying for months and years to build my own audience, I realized it's a very hard way to go about it. I tried creating a blog, a podcast, and an email newsletter. While I believe those are great and will give you exposure, it's a long road. People assume you can create a blog and people will come. That may work for some, but they are far and few between. Why not leverage other people's audiences?

When you've uncovered your message and you have a perspective to share, people who have built an audience want content to share. They want to highlight ideas, theories, and points of view with their community, and they look for people who have something interesting to say. Even better if your message is clear and they can see that you stand for something. When I got clear about what I wanted to share, people started to take notice. I pitched to podcasts, blogs, and conferences, and the momentum took off.

The best part is that you can consistently share the same message over and over again. I used to think you had to know a little about everything and share different ideas about different topics to look like an expert and knowledgeable person.

The opposite is true. When you think about it, an expert is someone who has intimate knowledge about a particular topic. When you go deep rather than wide on a topic, you'll position yourself as an expert and become a person of influence, getting called and requested to provide your point of view and share your knowledge. This is so freeing and far less stressful than trying to be and do it all. This is where the work on your zone of genius becomes relevant again. You don't have to share your message in the way I have or others have; you need to look at what works for you.

**Here are some ways you can leverage your message:**

- Participate in conferences that are linked to your message or have similar audiences.

- Offer to do webinars for organizations or groups with your audience.

- Leverage relationships with other leaders in your field to amplify your influence.

- Seek opportunities to share your message in your organization, like volunteering or hosting lunch-and-learn talks.

- Contribute to professional communities, panels, or online forums in your field.

- Volunteer in community projects or organizations.

- Pitch your ideas to established platforms like blogs, podcasts, or conferences that align with your message.

Sharing your message is empowering, as it connects you to your community, helps you attract the right opportunities, and amplifies your impact – whether you're leading a team, contributing as an employee, or building a business. I started by doing lunch – and – learn sessions at work. I shared what I was learning in my health coaching programme and began to champion the idea of workplace well-being practices. From there, things grew, and I started pitching webinars and articles to various groups. Soon, people started reaching out to me, and I was giving keynote speeches, delivering workshops, and now writing a book! I wasn't everywhere; I was just consistent with living my values, playing to my strengths, and in every appropriate conversation, I shared my message.

# Mapping Your Message

## Step 1: Identify the Right Spaces and Communities

First, brainstorm and research platforms, communities, or people that align with your message. Think about:

- Workplaces, local organizations, community groups, or events that are relevant to your message.

- People within your personal or professional network who can help you share your message or connect you to new opportunities.

**Questions to Ask:**

1. Who is already engaging with the type of audience or community I want to reach?

2. What spaces (workplace, local community, social circles) align with my message?

3. Are there professional associations, community centres, parenting groups, or volunteer organizations that resonate with my message?

**Action:**

- List at least five places (e.g. workplace departments, volunteer groups, local meetups) and five individuals (e.g. colleagues, leaders, mentors, or community organizers) that would be ideal for sharing your message.

## Step 2: Craft Your Pitch

Once you've identified the spaces and people, it's time to craft a compelling approach or pitch. Your pitch should clearly explain:

- What your message is and why it's valuable.

- Why their community or organization would benefit from your perspective.

- What you can contribute (e.g. hosting a workshop, leading a team project, speaking at an event, or offering volunteer support).

- A mutual benefit: how your message or contribution adds value to their goals or community.

## The Pitch Outline

1. **Introduction:** Briefly introduce yourself and your message.

2. **Value proposition:** Explain why your message is relevant and valuable to their community or organization.

3. **Contribution:** Offer a specific way you can contribute (e.g. leading a workshop, writing a newsletter article, or mentoring a group).

4. **Mutual benefit:** Highlight the benefit to them (e.g. fresh ideas, volunteer support, or added expertise).

5. **Call to action:** Ask if they'd be open to discussing your contribution further.

Here's a template you can use: My name is [Your Name], and I'm passionate about [your message]. I've been working on [short description of your work or experience]. I noticed your [community/organization] focuses on [related topic], and I believe my message about [topic] could add value. I'd love to contribute by [specific idea], which I think could benefit your group by [benefit to them]. Let me know if you'd be open to exploring this further!

## *Action*

· Write a pitch using the outline above for three spaces or individuals you've identified (e.g. a local community group, workplace project, or parenting circle).

No matter what your role is, begin sharing your message today. This is the first step to creating value by being of service to others. I never realized how valuable it could be to just share your message with someone who needs to hear it.

Sharing your message isn't just about advancing your goals, it's about making a meaningful connection with others, inspiring them, and making an impact in ways you may not even expect. Each time you share, you have the power to change a life.

Start with small steps like conversations. Each time you share your message, you strengthen your influence and move closer to living a life of significance. In the next, and final, chapter, we're going to explore how to move beyond just your message to create a legacy for yourself through assets that work for you and amplify your reach.

# 14

# Building Assets: Scaling Your Impact for Greater Reach

*The greatest use of life is to spend it on something that will outlast it.*

– William James

As you've journeyed through this book, you've worked on loving yourself, knowing yourself, and now we're on the final step: creating value. We've already started creating value by sharing our message with the world, but now it's time to go further and think about how we can create value that goes beyond our presence.

When I began reflecting on the idea of leaving a legacy, my children came to mind. The Self-love Mindset permeates my life, and my children will tell you that these are the very lessons and values I preach – and, hopefully, demonstrate. I thought about the one thing I wanted to leave with the world, but most importantly, with them. I always tell my children they need to love themselves first, because without self-love, they can't fully love anyone else. I tell them I love myself first, and that's why I can give them love from the overflow. I remind them to strengthen their strengths.

I've taken this idea of the Self-love Mindset as a parent seriously too. When it comes to self-awareness, I believe I'm the first to see their natural abilities – just as our parents or guardians may have noticed our gifts but perhaps didn't name them or give them much thought. My son loves mathematics and anything to do with numbers. I noticed this about him at a very young age. He's incredibly curious and asks deep, sometimes wild, questions. My daughter has been songwriting ever since she could speak. Every situation, happy or sad, became a song for her. She has a vivid imagination and truly belongs on a stage or should be writing a novel. Who knows?

I'm telling you this because I wanted to create something that my children can hold onto, something that shows I left a meaningful contribution in this world. I want them to hear my message every day: love yourself, know yourself, and then go out into the world and create value for yourself and others.

This is me creating value that extends far beyond my presence. In this chapter, we're going to explore how you can start thinking about creating assets in your own life – whether you're leading an organization, working within a team, or running your own business.

An asset is something you create once, but its value lives on. It's something that can continue to make an impact even when you're not there. For many people, a life of happiness and fulfilment isn't just about what they achieve at the moment; it's about the legacy they leave behind. Assets are a powerful way to build that legacy. This is where creating value for others also becomes creating value for yourself. I strongly believe in working smart, not hard. In fact, this became one of our company's core values. We advocate for a culture that allows people to work to their strengths in the zone of genius – where things should feel easy and flow, and most importantly, we make time for self-care.

Now, it's time to think about how you can expand your impact and work smarter. How can you serve and help more people without always being physically present? By creating assets that work for you.

An asset allows you to create value and make an impact even when you're not directly involved. It's about finding ways to continue contributing to others without constantly exchanging your time for effort. When you create assets, you're doing just that.

Assets can take many forms, such as writing a book, developing a programme, building a website, organizing a community group, or creating a guide or resource that others can benefit from. The possibilities are endless.

When you create assets, you:

- **Stop exchanging time for effort:** You allow yourself the freedom to create more and enjoy life without always needing to be present to make an impact.

- **Give people different ways to connect with you:** Some people may want personal interaction, while others might prefer reading your work, watching a video, or engaging with a self-paced course.

- **Increase your value:** By creating an asset once, you can benefit from it multiple times. This gives you more time and energy to develop additional resources for your community.

- **Shift from a time-based to an asset-based mindset:** Just like investing in something that grows over time, your assets have value that can continue to benefit others (and you) without needing to constantly reinvest time.

- **Create something valuable:** Whether it's a book, a resource guide, a procedure, or a programme, you now have something of value that can be shared with others, whether for free or in exchange for something else of value.

# Steps to Creating Your Own Assets

1. **Identify the Core of Your Message**

   The first step is to get clear on what part of your message can become a lasting resource. Is it a set of insights from your personal journey that you want to share in a book, like I'm doing here? Is it a process you've developed that could help others improve their health or business? Or maybe it's creating a space for a community to grow and learn together.

An important part of this is to see where you could be of most value to your audience. When I started sharing the work I was doing, I was leaning into the wellness practices I had learned. I was coaching clients, doing yoga classes (as I had become a certified teacher), and doing energy work. But I didn't enjoy that, and it began to feel like one of those burnout skills. I wasn't meant to be doing that part of the work. I wasn't leveraging my strengths, which were being creative, communicating, and breaking down bigger concepts and ideas.

On top of that, I didn't need to do all the things. I'm sharing the ideas and concepts, and you'll likely walk away from this book with aha moments – well, at least I hope you will. But there are other people I collaborate with who can go even deeper in each of these areas. This was a very freeing realization for me. I didn't need to become the authority on each of these pillars. I could share my approach, experiences, and resources by pulling them together in a way that someone can see the big picture and start their own journey.

2. **Choose the Format That Suits You**

You don't need to force yourself into a format that doesn't resonate with you. Think about your strengths:

- If you're a writer, consider starting with a blog, eBook, or a guide.

- If you're a speaker, a podcast, video series, or webinars might be the way to go.

- If you love mentoring, you might build a coaching programme, create a community group, or develop a workshop that can be delivered repeatedly.

- If you like teaching: A self-paced course, a local support group, or a step-by-step guide that others can follow.

- If you're process-driven: A framework, process, or method you've developed that others can use to improve their lives or work.

- If you like a community: Building a digital or in-person community that continues to grow and support its members.

The beauty of creating assets is that they allow you to serve others without always being directly involved. They keep working for you, and more importantly, for the people you're trying to help.

3.  **Start Small and Refine**

    You don't need to create a masterpiece right away. Start small, maybe with a simple guide or an introductory blog post, and refine it as you go. Just like with sharing your message, you'll gather feedback and evolve the asset over time. The key is to begin. I started with a presentation. That evolved into a workshop and speeches, then articles, then a small guide, a journal, and now a book. I'm sure I will create more assets as I go, but the key to working smart is that I'm not reinventing the wheel. I'm building on what I have.

4.  **Iterate and Improve**

    Once you've created your first asset, it's easier to refine and build more. Your first book can evolve into a course. Your community group might grow into a nationwide network. The possibilities expand as your assets start to take shape.

# Amplifying Your Assets

The next step is to help your assets reach the people who need them most. You've already learned about leveraging other people's platforms to share your message; now, you'll do the same with your assets.

Use platforms that allow you to distribute your assets widely. If you've written a book, publish it online. If you've built a course, share it through an e-learning platform.

Collaborate with others in your field who can help you promote your work. Keep sharing, and the impact will grow.

Ultimately, creating assets is about more than scaling your impact. It's about building a legacy. A legacy doesn't need to be grand to be significant. It can be as simple as a community you've nurtured or as large as a movement you've inspired. When you create assets, you're ensuring that your message continues to serve others, even when you're no longer actively involved.

With all of that said, it's still important to maintain the balance between personal connection and asset building. You don't need to stop engaging with people. In fact, your assets will only grow stronger when rooted in real, meaningful relationships.

The journey you've been on throughout this book, from loving yourself to sharing your message and creating assets, has been about building a life of significance. You're using your strengths to be of service to others around something that matters to you.

By creating assets, you're not just adding value to your own life, but to the lives of others. You're leaving behind something that will continue to inspire, educate, and support others for years to come.

Creating your legacy starts now.

It begins with loving yourself.

# Recap of Pillar 3: Creating Value

In Pillar 3, you move from internal growth to external impact by mastering your message, sharing it strategically, and creating assets that scale your influence. These focus areas guide you in becoming a person of significance, using your strengths and experiences to create lasting value for yourself and others. Through this process, you not only build a fulfilling life but also leave a legacy that continues to inspire and serve beyond your presence.

## *Master Your Message*

- Your message is the foundation of the value you create. It reflects your strengths, values, and the unique perspective you bring to the world.

- Crafting a powerful personal message is about identifying what truly matters to you and what you stand for. It's the guiding principle that influences all your actions.

- A well-defined message gives you clarity, focus, and purpose, helping you make decisions that align with your values and attract the right opportunities.

## *Share Your Message*

- Sharing your message is key to creating value for others. It allows you to build meaningful connections and reach the people who need to hear your message.

- You don't need to be everywhere; focus on the spaces and communities that resonate with your message. By sharing your story, insights, and experiences, you naturally attract the right opportunities and create a positive impact.

- Leverage platforms that already have your target audience, such as podcasts, blogs, or conferences, to amplify your message and extend your influence.

## *Create Assets*

- Creating assets is about building something that continues to provide value even when you're not present. Assets can be books, courses, programmes, or even community groups.

- Assets allow you to scale your impact, providing ongoing value without needing to exchange time for effort constantly.

- By developing assets, you create a legacy that can inspire, educate, and support others long after you've moved on from the initial creation, ensuring your message and value live on.

# Resources

## Assessments

### Myers-Briggs Type Indicator (MBTI)

A widely known personality assessment that categorizes individuals into 16 different personality types based on preferences in how they perceive the world and make decisions.

Website: www.myersbriggs.org

### Gallup StrengthsFinder (CliftonStrengths)

This tool helps you identify your top strengths and talents so you can build on them personally and professionally.

Website: www.gallup.com/cliftonstrengths

### DISC Personality Assessment

A behavioural assessment tool that examines how individuals communicate and interact with others, focusing on four traits: dominance, influence, steadiness, and conscientiousness.

Website: www.discprofile.com

## YouMap

Created by Kristin A. Sherry, YouMap helps individuals identify their unique strengths, values, motivating skills, and personality-based interests. This assessment and the book by the same name provide a detailed approach to self-awareness and personal development.

Website: www.myyoumap.com

## Enneagram of Personality

The Enneagram is a system that describes nine personality types, each with unique patterns of thinking, feeling, and behaving. It helps you understand your core motivations and potential areas for growth.

Website: www.enneagraminstitute.com

## 16Personalities

A free, accessible version of the MBTI that also incorporates elements of other personality theories. It gives a detailed breakdown of your personality type and provides tips for personal development.

Website: www.16personalities.com

## Entrepreneur Dynamics

A system designed specifically for entrepreneurs and leaders to help them identify their 'entrepreneurial profile'.

This tool provides insights into how you and your team can add the most value to your organization based on your natural strengths, focusing on eight different profiles, such as the Creator, Star, Supporter, and Deal Maker.

Website: www.geniusu.com/dynamics

**Marcus Buckingham's StandOut Assessment**

Based on the work of Marcus Buckingham, StandOut helps you discover your key strength roles and how to leverage them in your work and life. It's designed to identify your top two 'strength roles' to help you contribute effectively in teams and take your leadership to the next level.

Website: www.marcusbuckingham.com/standout

# Meditation and Mindfulness Resources

1. **Headspace**

   An app that offers guided meditation and mindfulness exercises to help reduce stress, improve focus, and connect with your inner self.

   Website: www.headspace.com

2. **Insight Timer**

   A free app with a large library of guided meditations, music, and talks on mindfulness and well-being.

   Website: www.insighttimer.com

3. **Calm**

   This app offers guided meditations, sleep stories, and relaxation techniques to help you manage stress and focus on well-being.

   Website: www.calm.com

# Gratitude and Journaling Tools

1. **The Five-minute Journal**

   A simple guided journal that helps you build a habit of gratitude and reflection in just five minutes a day.

   Website: www.intelligentchange.com

2. **Reasons to Feel Good Journal**

   A journal designed to encourage a mindset of intention and appreciation, helping you focus on what makes you feel good each day. It offers guided prompts to nurture a habit of gratitude and positivity.

   Website: www.lauriannainsworth.com

# Bibliography

Brown, Brené. *Daring Greatly: How the Courage to Be Vulnerable Transforms the Way We Live, Love, Parent, and Lead*. Gotham Books, 2012.

Chamine, Shirzad. *Positive Intelligence: Why Only 20% of Teams and Individuals Achieve Their True Potential and How You Can Achieve Yours*. Greenleaf Book Group Press, 2012.

Dweck, Carol S. *Mindset: The New Psychology of Success*. Random House, 2006.

Eurich, Tasha. *Insight: The Surprising Truth About How Others See Us, How We See Ourselves, and Why the Answers Matter More Than We Think*. New York: Crown Business, 2017.

Garnett, Laura. *Find Your Zone of Genius: Break Free from Burnout, Reduce Career Anxiety, and Make the Work You're Doing Matter by Making Your Job the Right Job for You*. Naperville, IL: Simple Truths, 2020.

Garnett, Laura. *The Genius Habit: How One Habit Can Radically Change Your Work and Your Life*. New York: Sourcebooks, 2019.

Hargrave, Tad. *Marketing for Hippies: Master Your Message.* Edmonton: Marketing for Hippies Press, 2021.

Hay, Louise L. *You Can Heal Your Life.* Hay House, 1984.

Hendricks, Gay. *The Big Leap: Conquer Your Hidden Fear and Take Life to the Next Level.* San Francisco: HarperOne, 2009.

Huffington, Arianna. *Thrive: The Third Metric to Redefining Success and Creating a Life of Well-Being, Wisdom, and Wonder.* Harmony Books, 2014.

Kipp, Mastin. *Claim Your Power: A 40-Day Journey to Dissolve the Hidden Blocks That Keep You Stuck and Finally Thrive in Your Life's Unique Purpose.* Hay House Inc., 2017.

LaPorte, Danielle. *The Desire Map: A Guide to Creating Goals with Soul.* Sounds True, 2014.

Maxwell, John C. *The Power of Significance: How Purpose Changes Your Life.* Center Street, 2017.

Pink, Daniel H. *Drive: The Surprising Truth About What Motivates Us.* New York: Riverhead Books, 2009.

Sherry, Kristin A. *YouMap: Find Yourself. Blaze Your Path. Show the World!* CreateSpace Independent Publishing Platform, 2018.

Tolle, Eckhart. *The Power of Now: A Guide to Spiritual Enlightenment.* New World Library, 2004.

# Index